Best l

Keith

Sept. '15.

CW00493502

CONDEMNATION TO COMMENDATION

by

Keith How

and Mick Hart

(C) Keith How

Published by

SE11 Books

CONDEMNATION TO COMMENDATION

First paperback edition printed 2015 in the United Kingdom

ISBN 978-0-9933179-0-3

Published by SE11 Books

For more copies of this book, please email:-
se11books@yahoo.com

Cover design by Philip Thomas
studio@piptom.com

Printed in Great Britain by bookprintinguk.com

Although every precaution has been taken in the preparation of this book, the publisher and author assume no responsibility for errors or omissions. Neither is any liability assumed for damages resulting from the use of this information contained herein.

DEDICATIONS AND THANKS

For my father Dennis and my late mother Joan, for their love and guidance. For my wife Lesley, for everything and my boys, Nicki and Chris for the continuing joy they bring to my life.

Also, special thanks to Mark 'Mumper' Baxter for his advice and encouragement and Philip Thomas for his fabulous design skills.

Keith How

For my family, for their loyalty and love. Also for all those who have taken part in KeepOut - The Crime Diversion Scheme, both past and present.

Mick Hart

CHAPTER ONE
SOWING THE SEEDS

1938 and despite the beautiful early summer days, London was still feeling the effects of the Great Depression. Everybody had felt it's effects to some extent. The 30's was a decade that had seen industry devastated, particularly in the north of England. Over 200 Shipbuilders from a town called Jarrow set off on an ill-fated march, which has gone down in history known as 'The Jarrow March', to the Palace of Westminster as a protest, such was the extreme poverty pervading in the north-east. Unfortunately the government at the time didn't seem too impressed with their efforts, as little was done to ease their plight, other than them being given a pound each for their train fare back home! The depression had a slightly milder effect in London and the south east, however, no doubt hardships were still being felt. I would guess my family, (then living in Ealing Road, Wembley) consisting of my mother and father, George and Elizabeth, (known as Betty) Hart and my eldest brother Peter, seven years old, were no different to most working class families and were feeling the pinch financially. Particularly as my father, I was to find out later, was more likely to risk his money on a horse than put food on the table. I'm sure my poor mother did her best to keep her family fed and clothed under these circumstances, but this can't have been easy considering the economy at that time and my father's habits. Consequently, when I arrived on the 16th June of that year, my poor Mum's burden must have increased somewhat. I was named Michael George Hart. We were still living in Wembley when the war started the year after my birth and my younger brother Bob was born there in 1940. Dad had now been conscripted into the Army and with Mr. Hitler doing his very best to flatten London, Mum decided evacuation was the best option for her family. We were fairly fortunate, as Mum's sister Alice lived in Wales, so Mum, myself and my two brothers went there as a family unit, rather than us kids being sent away alone.

I'm sure evacuation caused a lot of family heartache, but it was considered necessary to safeguard kids' welfare, future generations and the nation's future at a difficult time. However, even though many London kids loved the experience of leaving home (and for most children this was probably for the first time) and having the time of their lives in the country, this wasn't always the case. It's been well documented that some poor London kids were fostered out with families who, in many cases, didn't really want to take them in and the youngsters suffered badly because of it.

Taking an evacuee in wasn't a choice, if the authorities said you were to take a young lad or girl in, then you took them in or risk prosecution. Stories of cruelty, near starvation diets and slave labour have since come to light. Luckily this didn't apply to us as Mum was with us all the way, not that I remember too much about it at such a young age. We lived in a small town called Treharris, near Methyr Tydfil and thinking back now, well over seventy years later, I seem to recall my very first, vague memories are of going with someone, (maybe my brother Peter) to salvage remnants of coal from a local slag heap, also I have hazy recollections of spending some time on a farm nearby.

Throughout my time in Wales, I didn't attend school, I've no idea why this was. Treharris was a very small town at that time, maybe the equally small schools had closed down for the duration of the war or maybe Mum just didn't send me! Whatever the reason, when we all left Wales to return to London at the end of the war I was seven years old and hadn't had a single day's schooling.

Large sections of London had been devastated while we had been away and our little house in Ealing Road was no exception. Communications were pretty non-existent back then, other than letter and as Mum had not received one, we had no prior knowledge of our house being razed to the ground until we were stood in the street looking at what was left of it. We must have been a sorry and pitiful sight, with poor Mum and Peter crying their eyes out at the realisation of what this meant, myself and Bob not fully understanding, but crying because they were!

Obviously we weren't alone in this situation and there just wasn't enough emergency housing to go around and the authorities must have been under immense pressure to find shelter for large numbers of families. Dad was still away doing his bit in the Army at this time, so it was left to poor Mum to try to salvage something for us and it transpired that the only available accommodation for us initially, was in an air raid shelter. These places were pretty basic even for overnight stays during the bombing, but for a family to live there full-time was terrible. The lack of decent washing and toilet facilities and the sheer number of people down there made the place a complete dump. Families sleeping side by side in massively overcrowded conditions seemed a world away from our time in Treharris.

What an introduction to life back in London! It must have been hell for Mum, having to suffer her family being in that situation and feeling totally helpless, unable to do anything to ease our plight. I didn't realise at the time just how bad it was, I was seven years old and to a lad of that age, it seemed such an adventure, what seven year old wouldn't be thrilled to be living in an underground tunnel.

Fortunately we weren't there too long, I think it was only a matter of a week or two until they found us another house in the Wembley area which we were to share with another family.

We were in the larger, upstairs section and the other, smaller family were to live downstairs. They were nice people, the Swindlehursts, their young son who was about the same age as myself was named Colin. He was a good lad and we got along well, but unfortunately poor Colin was born with a dodgy eye, it was totally white and had no colour to the iris at all.

Shortly after we moved in, the electric lights fused and his mother went to the cupboard where the fuse box was sited, in an attempt to correct the problem. Colin had gone with her to help and I'd come out onto the landing to see what was occurring. His mother was using a candle to see whilst she changed the fuse wire as myself and Colin watched on. She turned around to ask Colin to pass a screwdriver and a big blob of molten wax dripped onto his good eye. He screamed and looked at me, as if looking to me for help. The sight of this poor little sod, who now had TWO white eyes, totally spooked me out. It was like something from a horror film, I subsequently screamed and ran. His poor mother didn't have a clue what was going on. I could still hear poor Colin's screams as I ran into my bedroom.

Dad was demobbed shortly after we settled there and we returned to some semblance of normal life, as best we could. My father's time in the services hadn't stopped his love of gambling and this also spread to him owning a share in a couple of greyhounds that were kept in kennels at a place called Probert's in Wembley. He had me raiding all the pig-bins for waste food scraps to take over to dogs. I'm pretty sure he made no real profit from them though, or if he did I'm pretty sure Mum or us boys didn't see benefit from it.

Rationing was still in force at that time and good food was scarce. I have a distinct memory of always feeling hungry, even after dinner, our main meal of the day. I'd arrived home one day and looked into the larder, looking for a snack or something and it was empty, completely bare. Old Mother Hubbard had nothing on us!

There was a grocer's shop near our house and it suddenly occurred to me "why don't I come back when the shop is shut and help myself"? I've no idea where this thought came from or why, but it seemed the perfect solution to my constant feelings of hunger. I'm not making excuses for my behaviour, even at the young and irresponsible age of eight years old, but I feel it had a major bearing on it.

So, I set about my mission. As we went to bed that very evening, I told my young brother Bob (who I shared a bedroom with) about my plan and asked him to wake me up at 1a.m., with the promise of a treat for his efforts. How I expected him to be able to be awake at that time to rouse me from my slumbers, I've no idea. We then settled down to some shuteye and sure enough, as planned, he woke me at the arranged time and then promptly received a bollocking from me for waking me in the middle of the night, until I remembered why!

I upped out of bed, put my clothes on over my pyjamas, grabbed a bag for the gear, crept downstairs and left the house. As I pulled the door too, I looked up and down the street, not a soul, good, I set off quietly towards the shop. I had no real idea of how I was going to get in, however, on arrival there was a small vent window open above the main door and I carefully dragged a dustbin over to directly underneath it, shinned up and squeezed myself in through the small gap. Once inside I stuffed my bag with groceries, butter, milk, cheese, whatever I could find, not forgetting some chocolate for young Bob and set off back home. Our house front door was slightly ajar, just as I'd left it...in...pushed it shut gently...softly upstairs...into my room and back into my warm bed. I don't reckon I was gone for more than fifteen minutes, all done and dusted, but my brother Bob was fast asleep again. His chocolate treat could wait until tomorrow.

I put the stuff I'd thieved under the bed and took it down to Mum in the morning. She was delighted and congratulated me! Make of that what you will, any psychologists reading this will probably be doing somersaults by now, but at that time, all I knew was that my Mum was pleased with me and I had some decent grub to eat.

Sure, she should have given me a walloping and made me take the stuff back, but she didn't. Maybe my Mum's situation of struggling to feed a family under the restrictions of rationing and my Dad's gambling contributed to her actions, I don't know. Maybe it was just that she saw nothing wrong in thieving. Either way I had discovered that even at the tender age of eight years old, I'd enjoyed the experience. It wasn't just the fact that my actions had improved our lack of food and my subsequent hunger, the very act of thieving had given me a thrill. So much so that I returned to the shop on several further occasions!

I'd finally started school shortly before this time at Park Lane Junior School, not that I thought too much of it. I can vividly remember running home after just a few minutes of the first day with my younger brother Bob and on numerous other occasions. However, one incident from that time that has totally stuck in my mind is of me helping myself to a pound note out of our teacher Ms. Staver's handbag that she'd left on the desk one day.

Now, when I look back at myself at that very young age, it baffles me why thieving opportunities like this would even enter my mind, almost as second nature. I'm pretty sure that my parents showing such pleasure at me returning home with groceries on that first occasion must have some bearing on it. Anyway, I treated three of my pals to toy trumpets with the cash from my poor teacher's purse.

Spurred on by my successes at the shop (and school), I was now
constantly on the look out for further thieving opportunities and it didn't
take me long to stumble onto one.

While out and about with my mates, I noticed the unloading of stacks of
boxes from trains onto the platform of the nearby railway station. Later
that day they were loaded onto a lorry to continue their journey. Having
no idea what was in them didn't matter to me, whatever it was meant
money and money meant nice things! There must have been something
inside me, to make an eight year old lad associate seeing boxes being
unloaded from a train into a thieving opportunity. There are theorists
who have suggested that some people are just BORN naughty, I'm not
sure on that one. However, it can't have been every young lad who
thought my way.

Anyway, at the far end of the platform was a fence separating the
railway tracks from the street. I climbed over this fence, then under the
overhang of the platform into a safe recess away from the tracks and
crawled along unnoticed until I reckoned I was roughly at the area of the
platform where the boxes were stacked. From this vantage point,
ensuring no trains were coming, I could peer up, making sure I was in
the right place, alongside the goodies and checking the coast was clear,
clamber up onto the platform and help myself to these boxes and their
contents.. I think these boxes were destined for the shelves of
Woolworth's or somewhere similar, as the goods were generally things
like cheap purses and wallets. Once again, when I took these bits and
pieces home I was congratulated by Mum and Dad, who then took them
into their respective workplaces to sell onto their colleagues. Dad was
working as a storekeeper at that time and Mum worked for Goodman's,
the electronics company. I was given a few shillings for my troubles and
encouraged to go back for more. These railway platform jobs lasted a

while until the platform staff realised something was amiss and thought it wise to store the in-transit goods elsewhere, away from thieving little toe rags like me.

My stealing continued throughout my junior school years, then my first arrest occurred at the age of eleven. My brother Bob and I were mucking about in the street, when a horse and cart passed by with a large load of bananas on board. We'd heard of bananas and seen these exotic fruit in books, but never had the chance of a taste. Temptation (and curiosity) got the better of us, so we followed it to a greengrocers shop nearby. We watched as the fruit was unloaded into the shop and decided we'd come back after closing time to see what was possible. As arranged, we returned later and I climbed into the shop through a small, open window, leaving Bob outside to keep watch and I threw him a banana to eat. I tried this unknown fruit as well and loved it! As I was loading my bag, Bob called out "there's someone coming", thinking he was just panicking I took no notice, I just threw him another banana. The next thing I knew, a copper came in, his torch shining straight onto my face, nicked. We both appeared at Wealdstone Juvenile Court the very next day charged with Simple Larceny, both found guilty and fined 20 shillings each. They had actually brought the discarded skins from the bananas we'd been unable to resist tasting, as evidence! When they were produced, the whole court burst into laughter as young Bob piped up with, "The fine should only be 10 shillings, half of my banana was bad". Nevertheless, bad banana or not, my criminal record had it's first entry.

My gaining a criminal record at such a young age was probably the least of my parents worries, (that is, if they worried about it at all) as shortly after my appearance at court I became seriously ill.

At a loose end one day and with none of my pals around, I decided to take myself off on a cycle ride and as the weather was nice, thought Rickmansworth Lakes (now known as Rickmansworth Aquadrome) was a fitting destination. This was a beautiful landscaped area with a series of large lakes. Now, Rickmansworth is a fair distance (for cycling for a young lad) from north London and on arrival, sweating from my exertions, decided a refreshing dip was what I needed. The water felt great as I swam and splashed around for a while, then laid myself down in the gardens to enjoy the afternoon sunshine. I then cycled back home, having enjoyed my day out. I awoke the following day feeling terrible. Mum didn't like the look of me, so took me straight off to the doctor's. After a very minor consultation, the GP decided it was nothing to worry about and sent me off home, issuing Mum a prescription for a sleeping draught intended to give me a restful night's sleep and hopefully, back to normal the next day. The intended result didn't occur, I broke into a serious fever during the night and was rushed into hospital. I was moved into an isolation ward as a precaution, this ward contained several glass cubicles, with a bed and a small cabinet in each. I was put to bed inside one of these units, not really knowing who I was, or indeed where I was. The only time I recall actually being fully awake was when a needle was inserted into my back for a lumber puncture. The size of this needle, which I asked to see after the injection, was vast. I wished I'd never asked! The fluid drained from the needle was analysed and polio was diagnosed. Apparently, Mum and/or Dad were at my bedside constantly and because of the contagious nature of the disease wore large gowns and masks while with me. After 17 days and nights I had managed to shake it off and was discharged from hospital, fortunately with no lasting after effects. I suspect that my swim in the lake at Rickmansworth was the cause of my illness. Mum told me that the doctors at the hospital had informed her that it was touch and go for some time, whether I was actually going to pull through. It was only then that I realised the seriousness of my illness, as I had been more or less 'out of it' for the majority of my time in isolation. I believe that Polio is spread in water and I can recall seeing many dead fish during my swim. I'd probably swallowed a mouthful or two and that was that. I spent a further short period recuperating at home, but fortunately, was soon up and running again.

It was around this time that I began to realise that aside from him flogging off my ill-gotten gains, Dad was also a thief himself. I can't recall who he was working for at that time, but amongst the goods under his supervision as a storekeeper were rolls of phosphor bronze metal. In addition to 'supervising' these rolls of valuable metal, he also liked to bring them home! Dad used to place these rolls over his head like a very heavy scarf and then conceal them on his journey home, by wearing an enormous black macintosh. It was then my job to break up the metal into smaller pieces to disguise the fact it had been stolen. I used to smash away at this stuff for hours and then push it round (on multiple trips) on a little barrow to the local scrap metal dealers to sell. I'd take the cash from this enterprise back to Dad and once again, I'd then be given another couple of bob and Dad would gamble his share away again.

I know now looking back, that my parents obviously have to take some sort of responsibility for the way my life was going. Okay, their jobs were poorly paid, money and food were scarce and my father's gambling habits didn't help, but the way I was encouraged along this path was very wrong. Some may call my parent's behaviour dysfunctional. Having said that, even at that young age I knew that thieving gave me a real buzz, I totally loved the thrill of it. I've heard it said that stealing can become addictive and I can totally relate to that.

I started at secondary school and aside from all the skulduggery, I began to take a real interest in boxing. I joined a good club in Ealing and showed a lot of promise even early on, which the coaches spotted and nurtured. After a period of training, which I really enjoyed, I began to box competitively with considerable success. An amusing incident occurred at one tournament early in my boxing career, (not that I saw the funny side of it at the time!) when upon arrival at the venue, my father took my kit into the changing room, ready for when I was to change for my bout. At the necessary time, I emptied (what I thought was) my bag to find a distinct lack of gloves, vest and shorts. The bag was full of ladies underwear! Someone must have had a similar looking bag on our bus journey and picked up the wrong one!. I managed to loan some kit and continue with my fight.

However much of a diversion the boxing was, it wasn't enough to keep me away from my criminal activities, as around that time, Dad (setting me a great example again) started taking me out thieving with him. Breaking and entering was Dad's main game and I came in useful, being smaller and certainly more agile than my father. Climbing and squeezing through small gaps were no real problem for me. Anything and everything that could be nicked was fair game to myself and Dad. Whatever we managed to steal would be sold off and as usual, I was given no more than a few shillings each time we pulled off a job, Dad's gambling habits made sure of that.

This continued until I was nicked on a job, the old man managing to scarper, leaving me to take the rap! I was questioned as the Police were fairly positive that I wasn't alone, but I never mentioned Dad's involvement. Even at fourteen years old, I'd learnt that you never grass. I was fined 40 shillings for this offence.

Dad was still stealing the metal from his work at this time and had brought another load home. He told me not to bother with breaking this lot up as I usually did, but to take it around to my elder brother Peter's house, as he'd take it from us as it was, saving me the back-breaking work. Peter was married by now and living with his wife in rented rooms in Willesden. I carried the metal round there in a wooden case and as I arrived I saw two men leaving. Peter's wife let me in and looking flustered, blurted out "Did you see those two blokes leaving? They're Old Bill! They've got Peter down the nick. Quick, get the metal out of the case and hide it!"

I did as she said and at that precise moment, the door knocker sounded and the two coppers had returned. They asked me what was in the case I'd carried in. I told them it was empty and that I'd brought it round to carry some stuff back home. Obviously not believing me, they searched and found the metal. That was me nicked again and taken to Willesden Police Station. Upon arrival, the desk Sergeant took great delight in saying, " It looks as though the whole of your family collects metal, your brother's already in here on the same charge!" Once again I kept the old man out of it, telling them I found the metal. I received two years probation for this offence.

Away from the villainy with Dad, my amateur boxing career had been shaping up nicely. I had won the London Junior ABA (Amateur Boxing Association) Championships at Welterweight. One of my fondest memories from this time was fighting at the Toby Club on Mile End Road. On the same bill was a young Henry Cooper, who everybody knows now and also Dave Charnley, a talented English lightweight fighter who turned pro shortly after and had a very successful career. He became known as 'The Dartford Destroyer'.

I fought a young lad this particular evening, who was the Federation of Boy's Clubs Champion, I knocked him out in 40 seconds and on leaving the ring, there were loads of coppers watching the fight and apparently they'd all had a bet on me. One of them congratulated me and pushed a ten shilling note into my glove, saying "keep that quiet". Obviously as an amateur, no money should be received. That was the first and last time I got any money out of the Police! However, shortly after this I was concussed while sparring (unsupervised and without permission) with a heavyweight and was advised to stop boxing.

The thieving continued and around this time, I teamed up with one of my school pals, a lad called Ronnie Smith who was a very bright kid, always on the lookout for our next opportunity. We used to plan our afternoon and evening activities during our lunch breaks at school. On the whole, these after school outings consisted of shoplifting from local stores. However, one day he came in really excited about a new angle he'd thought up. He used to do a paper round and some of his deliveries were to shops, such as Curry's and Stone's. As he pushed the newspapers through the letterboxes of these stores, he'd noticed, sitting on the doormat, the many letters that the postman had delivered earlier. These stores were electrical retailers and at this time, the vast majority of working class people were not in a position to pay cash for these expensive purchases, so had to take out hire purchase agreements on their goods.

Also, very few people had bank accounts in those days, so young Ronnie had figured that perhaps the letters sat on their doormats contained cash or postal order payments from customers.

"Great, maybe they are" I said to Ronnie, "but we won't be able to reach them"! Ronnie was one step ahead of me here,

"You'll see" he said with a smirk and we arranged that I'd accompany him on his paper round the next day.

I met Ronnie early and we set off delivering newspapers. As we arrived at the first of these shops, Ronnie looked through the letterbox, the postman had been and loads of letters were sat inside. He then produced, from his paperbag, a bicycle pump with several of those flexible adaptors that screw onto the tyre valve, screwed together hanging from the end of the pump. This 3ft length of adaptors was then poked through the letter box until the end of the nozzle was on one of the letters, the pump was operated and as if by magic, the letter attached itself to the end and was pulled up, until it was near enough to the letterbox for me to poke my hand in and grab it! Lo and behold, the first letter out contained a postal order for a pound or two. Back in with the pump, some cash..and again! We had a nice few quid, but were careful enough to make sure we left some letters there, so as not to arouse suspicion, we wanted to come back again! And we did, many times!

Another of my partners in crime during my schooldays was Robert Isles. He hadn't really been involved in anything dodgy until I took him with me one day, when I planned to break into a shop. We managed to get in and came across a locked briefcase, which we forced open and to our delight, discovered seventy quid inside. This was around 1951 and that was serious money then and the next day treated ourselves to a lovely air rifle each. That night when returning home after an evening messing with our guns, decided it'd be good fun to shoot out all the street lamps. My old man saw us doing this and confiscated our guns. The next day he told us that the Police knew it was us who had shot out the lights and that to get us out of being arrested, he'd had to sell the guns to pay them off. The lying git had gambled the proceeds, as usual!

Around this time I begun to fully understand the extent of Dad's gambling. When I was younger, I had always thought that he was attempting to improve our lot by winning, therefore bringing some much needed cash into the household. As I got into my teenage years however, I realised that his gambling was doing no more than bringing more hardship to our already struggling family. On several occasions, I recall Dad arriving home late in the evening on payday and..surprise, surprise...his pay packet had mysteriously fallen out of his pocket on his way home. Mum probably even believed it on the first occasion. This caused rows between my parents, as obviously Mum had known about Dad's gambling habit for years and had probably heard every excuse in the book countless times.

I continued with my thieving throughout my schooldays and was always on the lookout for my next opportunity.

CHAPTER TWO
SEX AND THE ARMY

I left school in 1953, aged 15 and started my first job with an engineering company, as a trainee, which I really enjoyed. Machines and mechanics were something that had always interested me, so I got on well with my training and showed a lot of promise as an engineer, so much so that the management team there often said I could go all the way. If only I'd kept my head down and just got on with my work, who knows what different direction my life may have taken. The company was Funditor and they made machinery for the printing trade, I worked initially in the machine shop, however being the most junior member of staff, I was also a messenger and general dogsbody. The foreman regularly sent me on errands to a company in Farringdon with deliveries, being so young I could just about get away with half price fare on the train, but made sure I claimed the full adult rate from the company. So apart from a welcome respite from the factory floor, I also managed to supplement my meagre wages as well.

Shortly after starting work, I started going out with my first real girlfriend. I'd messed around with girls whilst at school, but Barbara was the first girl I slept with. She worked in a shoe shop in the market and I used to skive off work on pretence of a dentist appointment on a Wednesday afternoon, (her half-day off from work and her parents both out!) to go round to her place. She'd make me a cup of tea and as I took the last mouthful of tea, she used to nod her head in the direction of the bedroom! Young Barbara was a girl who certainly had an appetite for a bit of the other and as a young man starting out on his sexual adventure, who was I to complain? During one of our weekly sessions, she opened a drawer on her bedside cabinet and pulled out a massive dildo. I'd never seen one before and must have looked dumfounded and unsure of what to do with it. However, she soon demonstrated their usefulness, much to my delight! I seem to recall we went out for about a year and half, but like most romances between kids of that age it fizzled out.

Even though I was progressing well at work with my training and becoming quite a skilled engineer, I was still inclined to supplement my wages with various bits of skulduggery. One Saturday evening, as a pal and myself were leaving a cinema, we spotted a motorcycle sitting at the kerb. Reckoning there could be a few quid involved, I decided to take it. Having no idea of how to start it without a key, I jumped on and began to roll it down the hill, the cinema being conveniently situated at the top of an incline. I'd progressed about a hundred yards when a man jumped off the kerb and grabbed hold of me. He explained that he was a Policeman and asked what was going on. I quickly came back with a cock and bull story about this being my friend's motorbike and that he was in the cafe at the top of the hill. He pulled me from the bike and holding me by the arm, marched me back up the hill to check the validity of my story. Halfway back up, I decided to make a run for it and struggled free of the copper's grip and had it away. Thinking it wise not to try and find my pal, I headed straight home to find the Police waiting for me. My "friend" had been grabbed by another plainclothes Policeman and had given him my name and address on the promise of not being charged himself. I was charged with taking a motor vehicle without consent, no insurance and assaulting a police officer. The assault charge was because I had broken free of his grip on my arm! A five pound fine was imposed for the assault and twelve months conditional discharge for the other offences.

A more successful venture with two wheels surfaced shortly after this when my younger brother Bob and I started thieving bicycles, nobody seemed to lock them up in those days, the fools! We used to swap wheels and frames from one bike to another, repaint them and sell them on, earning us a nice little profit. My skills as an engineer certainly came in handy in this enterprise.

My job at Funditor continued with further spells in other sections, i.e. tool shop, the machine shop and the experimental department and I thoroughly enjoyed the experience.

There were some real characters working with me, one young fella who went by the nickname of 'Muffin' worked in the fitting department. Why he was called this, I've no idea, but poor old Muffin wasn't the sharpest tool in the box, to put it mildly. He was as gormless as they come and unfortunately was the victim of any willing joker, myself included.

One such incident that springs to mind, was probably a bit cruel thinking back now, but at the time seemed a real laugh. Poor Muffin only had one tie, a red one, which he wore day in, day out, probably for years on end. Now this tie was absolutely filthy, it was covered in grease and grime collected over God knows how long, so much so that you could only just about tell the colour. Due to the state of Muffin's tie, it was often the topic of conversation. One day he came into the tool shop where I was working at the time and unfortunately for him, someone had just handed in a large set of scissors, which were still in my hand. As he stood there looking at me, trying to get his words out, all I could focus on was this manky old red tie and without thinking, I reached out and cut his tie off just below the knot. Poor old Muffin's mouth dropped open, he was silent for a moment or two then burst into tears and ran off. He soon grassed me up and I received a bollocking for my actions. Word soon spread around the firm about the incident and after everybody had a good laugh about the famous 'Muffin Red Tie Incident', out of sympathy to the poor sod he was presented with a new tie by almost everybody in the company. Muffin was now swimming in ties, a fresh new tie almost every day. So really, I done him a favour!

Unfortunately my time there came to an end when I was conscripted into the army, (national service in those days!) in 1957. I was sent to Aldershot, to the RASC (Royal Army Service Corps) where my training commenced as a Storekeeper. Even though the RASC's main duties were in transport, I was disqualified for driving at that time, (don't ask, another disagreement about my motoring habits!) so couldn't be used as a driver. I also trained with further periods at Farnborough and Bulford.

Upon completion of my training later that same year I was shipped off to Singapore on active service, where I was stationed at 4 Supply Reserve Depot (4RSD). As I'd trained as a storekeeper I was put in charge of the armoury as the Unit Armourer. The 4RSD was situated some miles away from the armoury, so I only actually went to base once a week to pick up my wages,(the mind blowing figure of one pound and seven shillings with an extra one pound and thirteen shillings overseas allowance!) My duties at the armoury finished at midday and having plenty of spare time on my hands, I enrolled on as many courses as I could. I trained in Life Saving which I passed with a bronze medallion. I flew through the Army Education Certificate with ease and as strange as it seems to me now, I also passed a square bashing course! My success in these courses gave me the qualifications of a Staff Sergeant, even though at that time I was lowly Private Hart. However after one year's service I made Lance Corporal. While serving in Singapore I became involved in all kinds of sport, most of them new to me. There were some weights on the balcony of the billet and I enthusiastically joined my colleagues in a daily workout. A short walk away was the most beautiful swimming pool surrounded by palm trees in the grounds of the Sandy Soldiers Home, which was for the use of all Service personnel, but mainly by troops on leave from fighting communist terrorists in the Malayan jungle. I became a very good swimmer and went on to represent the Army at Diving and 100 yards Backstroke, I was also selected for the Army Water Polo Team.

My Company Sergeant Major, CSM Frankland, who I was directly responsible to, was a small bore rifle champion. He introduced me to this great sport and I took to it like a duck to water. He was an excellent shot and his instruction was first class, soon he'd trained me up to a very high standard. We both went on to represent the Army in many competitions, often shooting against the Gurkha Rifles who were stationed near to 4SRD and generally beating them convincingly.

Athletics were encouraged in the army as a means to general good fitness and I became heavily involved, representing them at the 440 yards and Shot Put. As I mentioned previously I had stopped boxing at sixteen years of age on advice, however I guess boxing was in my blood and when was asked to represent the Army I didn't refuse. I thought it best not to mention that I'd been told not to box again! I won every contest that I entered.

Saturday night was our big night out and me and the guys in my unit would get a taxi into the local town. The Union Jack Club would be our first port of call for a few cold beers before going on to a place called 'The Happy World'. This was a massive fenced compound where enjoyment was the order of the night. There were all kinds of fairground attractions and many bars frequented by the town's young prostitutes. Before going to Singapore we were warned about sexually transmitted diseases that were rife in hot countries. We were also shown films of people who had been infected with such diseases, the awful images from these films stuck in my head and as much as I was tempted, thankfully kept me away from ever exposing myself to such dangers. A favourite attraction of ours at Happy World was the taxi dancing bandstand. You paid a few cents for each dance where you could choose your partner from a selection of generally lovely, Chinese or Malayan girls. Within reason the girl you danced with had to follow your every move. A couple of times one of my close mates Chalky White, would get thrown off the Joggit, as it was called, for getting far too familiar with the girls. Dancing with the girls was what you paid for, not kopping a feel at the same time! Tattoos have always been popular with servicemen and there was certainly no shortage of parlours around Happy World. Many of my pals became well inked while out on a boozy nights and try as they did, had no success in persuading me to join them.

Due to my heavy involvement in sporting activities, I became the unit Physical Training Instructor, (PTI) while also continuing my duties in the armoury and loved every minute of my two years in the Army. However, when the CSM came to me with some papers to sign on for seven years, attractive as it seemed, I was pretty homesick and getting home seemed my main priority. The CSM said I was a fool because I had great prospects, thanks to the many qualifications I'd gained in my relatively short time in the Army. Looking back now, he was absolutely right. Had I signed on I would have had a terrific future. But hindsight is a wonderful thing, if only I knew then what I know now! But no, I followed my all too youthful instinct to get back home to Blighty. I was discharged with an excellent service record and received the General Service Medal (Malaya), of which I am very proud.

Looking back now, many years later, I often wonder what course my life would have followed had I signed on for longer service, I feel pretty sure I wouldn't have continued into more serious crime. Life in the services is very disciplined, I loved it and was still young enough to change from my old ways. I hadn't had the slightest sniff of any trouble during my service. Opportunities for villainy were less prevalent in the Army and to be honest, with my day to day duties and sporting activities, I was far too busy and much less inclined to get involved in anything dodgy. I was sent back to the UK and I was immediately demobbed. The year was 1959.

CHAPTER THREE

BACK HOME

I arrived back in London and as much as I loved my time in the Army and particularly Singapore, it felt good to be home. Things had changed in the music scene while I'd been serving my country, Rock and Roll had arrived, with Bill Hayley's 'Rock Around The Clock' having hit the UK with a bang and the emergence of the Teddy Boy scene. Youngsters were making their mark and it was a whole new era.

Mum was pleased to see me and was delighted at the prospect of me living back in the family house. However, Dad was still Dad! Getting a job was my first priority, so firstly I decided to try my old employer Funditor.

They took me back on and I thought I'd soon be back enjoying my work there. Unfortunately my time in the open air of sunny Singapore had made me realise that being confined inside factory walls all day long wasn't for me. I managed to stick it out for a few weeks, but left when it became too much. Once again, thinking back to this period, maybe I should have signed back on with the Army for another term. It probably seems as though I was being too choosey, but in those days jobs seemed two-a-penny compared to the present time. So seeking a more outdoor lifestyle, I decided to try my luck in the building trade.

By now, Dad had finished at the company from where the metal thefts had taken place. I think it was more a case of leaving before he got tumbled, rather than just deciding to move on of his own accord. He was now employed as a painter and decorator and managed to get me taken on by his company as a trainee. I soon realised that this work was more to my liking and settled into learning the decorating trade. I was really keen to get on and as I had with my previous engineering training, I progressed well, absorbing as much knowledge as I could. I had recently bought my first car, an Austin A40 Somerset and motored, on a daily basis up to Hemel Hempstead, where at that time many new housing and commercial developments were in progress. On these journeys to work, I gave a lift to three other painters on the same firm as myself. One of these men was the foreman, Ron, who became my mentor throughout my training. Ron was a great teacher and seemed to really enjoy passing on his vast knowledge of the decorating game. We got on famously, worked together well and I was soon picking up all the tricks of the trade. There was a great bunch of lads working on the developments at Hemel. Some of them were local people and I became friendly with many of them, some decorators like myself, but also from a whole multitude of other different trades. Whilst mixing with these guys, I managed to pick up tips and knowledge of their respective skills and soon considered myself a bit of a jack of all trades.

One trade which I managed to master fairly quickly was floor laying, which was useful as there was a massive supply of thermoplastic tiles on site, there for the taking. These floor tiles were extremely in vogue at this time, the in-thing. So, most evenings a box of these found their way into the boot of my car. I soon had enough to tile the hallway and toilet of Mum and Dad's flat. Mum was delighted and took great pride in bringing all her friends in to show off my handiwork. Pretty soon orders were coming in left right and centre for my floor laying services and products.

I think if you'd have checked inside the flats of our neighbourhood at that time, the vast majority of the rooms would have exactly the same flooring. They only had one colour scheme available to thieve! This became a real profit maker for me, not that any of it was saved, easy come, easy go as they say.

While out and about one evening, I bashed into an old pal of mine by the name of David Branch, (known as Twiggy, for obvious reasons) from my time at Funditor. He invited me to a British Legion Club in Wealdstone Lane, where he insisted the girls outnumbered the guys by three to one. This sounded interesting, and never one to turn down an opportunity, off we went. Twiggy was right, there were absolutely loads of girls. This became a regular haunt for us around this time and we jived the nights away to the popular sounds of the era. Little Richard, Fats Domino et al would be blasting out of the speakers and we all had a great time, fuelled by little more than Pepsi Cola. It all seems so innocent now looking back, but I'd never really been a boozer as such and I'm still not.

On one occasion, we met two girls there and after an evening of dancing and doing our best with our cheesy chat-up lines, they were up for a drive with us. We all piled into my car and set off for 'Lover's Lane'. The girls seemed perfectly fine with this and as soon as we parked up, the kissing and cuddling started. After a while, things started getting a bit more serious and I think Twiggy and I were both just about at the point of no return, when they was a loud tap on the (now very steamed up) window. The girls both jumped up with a start, pulling their draws up and their bra's down in the process. I opened the window, to be greeted with a Copper's torch shone straight in my face, he then diverted the torch beam inside the car, to see the girls trying to make themselves respectable.

"Everything alright here ladies?" he asked, a large grin on his face.
"Yes, fine", the girls replied in unison, their faces reddening by the second.
"Well, I'll leave you in peace then" he smirked as he walked off.

I'm sure the dirty old sod had been there for a while copping an eyeful, way before he banged on the window. Still, it livened up what was probably a boring night for him. Who said I never help the Police?

One night, as Twiggy and myself drove back from the club, I recognised two pretty girls walking along that we'd danced with earlier. Pointing them out to my pal, I said "I fancy the one in the yellow coat" and pulled the car over to the kerb alongside them.

After a few minutes of our wit and charm, they accepted the offer of a lift home. The girl who I'd taken a fancy to, who was called Wendy, unfortunately got into the car first, so ended up in the back with Twiggy and the other girl, Carol, in the front with me. Although I was a little disappointed that my first choice hadn't sat in the front with me, Carol was also very attractive, so who was I to complain. We drove on and our chat-up must have had some effect, as we ended up parked in the local lover's lane again. Once we were parked up away from prying eyes, myself and old Twiggy done our best to get what every young red bloodied male is out to get. Not that we were very successful. If anyone passing had sneaked a peek inside my car at that time, it would have looked like two all-in wrestling matches taking place. As hard as I tried to get my hand planted inside Carol's sweater, she was having none of it. Twiggy was no more successful in the back from what I could see. This continued until the silence was broken by Wendy,

"I don't let boys do that on the first night",old Twiggy came back with insistence,

"I'm not a fucking boy, I'm a man"!

All four of us burst into laughter, typical of Twiggy, he always was a funny sod. Anyway, we drove on and dropped the girls off home and watched them as they walked off, but Wendy, the girl in the yellow coat with the short dark hair, had made much more of an impression on me than Carol.

I went back to work on Monday, but the week dragged, as I longed for the weekend and our Saturday night at the British Legion Club. Wendy was stuck in my mind. Will she be there? Won't she? Will she make a bee-line for Twiggy? Do I think she'll fancy me? How will I persuade Twiggy to leave the coast clear for me? A thousand thoughts raced through my head all week long.

Eventually the weekend arrived and Twiggy and I arranged to meet for our trip to the club. I'd never felt this way about a girl before and on our drive there, I was praying that Twiggy would bring up the subject of the two girls we'd given a lift to, to give me the chance to tell him the situation. Pray as I might, Twiggy didn't mention them. Should I say something? Would it make me look a prat? Would it be uncool? Will Twiggy laugh at me? We pulled up outside the club and as I walked towards the entrance with my fingers crossed, urging Wendy to be there, I tried to persuade myself that even if she wasn't here, I'd still have a great night. It didn't work, I knew if she wasn't in the club, I'd be severely disappointed, not that I'd show it of course! We walked in and as we approached the bar, I resisted the temptation to swivel my head around to scan for Wendy, much as I wanted to. However, I scanned the club as best I could without making it look obvious. Twiggy and I bought our drinks and leant on the bar, me trying to look cool and nonchalant and again surveyed the club seeing who was in and who wasn't. There was no sign of Wendy...or Carol! Were they coming? Had we put them off? Twiggy still hadn't mentioned them, so it was down to me to bring the matter up without seeming too eager, too keen.

"I wonder if those two birds'll be here tonight?"

"Dunno" said Twiggy not sounding too bothered one way or the other.

Which was good news for me, he obviously hadn't given Wendy more than a moment's thought since last week. It probably wasn't more than a few minutes before Wendy and Carol walked in, but it seemed like hours. Twiggy hadn't noticed them, now was my chance, I walked over towards them with my heart in my mouth to say hello. Would they even remember me? Fortunately they did and we made small talk, "How was your week?", "How did you get here tonight?", the usual rubbish, until Carol shot off to the ladies and gave me the opportunity to speak to Wendy alone. I knew Carol wouldn't be gone long, so I'd have to come straight out with it. I asked her if we could meet one evening during the week for a drink. To my delight, she agreed and that was it, a date was fixed!

We had a great time and got on well. Wendy was very easy going and we enjoyed each other's company. We arranged to meet again and before long we were going steady, (a term we used in those days)! Wendy's parents were a funny couple though. Her mother Ivy, was a real character and somewhat absent minded, she could never remember anyone's name, (or maybe it was just me!) she always called me 'Thingy'. I was around there one day and while waiting for Wendy to finish getting ready for our date, Ivy asked if I'd like to see her chickens. I wasn't that fussed about seeing them, but feigning interest and not wanting to seem rude, said I'd love to. So she marches me out to the back yard and proudly shows off her chickens in a fenced off area, with a coop for egg laying. She seemed so enthusiastic, telling me how many eggs she'd get from these chickens, I tried to look interested and hoped she'd think I was genuine. A week or two later, while over at Maureen's house, out of politeness I asked Ivy how the chickens were getting along. As quick as you like she said, "those noisy gits....I got rid of them....I've got a load of tortoises now"!

It was as much as I could do to stop myself spitting out a mouthful of tea. What a replacement for chickens....tortoises. One day while I was visiting Wendy, alone in the front room with Ivy, she mentioned a woman who lived locally, called Mary, who was very promiscuous and that I should be careful as she'd more than likely make a play for me, given half the chance. Sounds interesting I thought, wonder if she's pretty? Lo and behold, later that day, I was dropping Wendy back home and as I was pulling the car into the kerb near her house, I noticed a woman sitting on her doorstep, her legs a yard apart and I could have sworn she was wearing no knickers. Needing to confirm this, I reversed the car a few yards for a second look....I was right...she wasn't, she had already noticed me looking her way on my first sighting, now she was staring me full in the face with a wry smile on her face! By now, I had suspected that this was Mary, which was confirmed by Wendy a second later,

"Drive on! That's Mary" she barked.

I said nothing and parked a bit further down the road. That was the only time I saw Mary, Wendy made very sure of that! I'm pretty sure that Ivy had learnt that her fears concerning Mary making a play for me were correct as well.

In complete contrast to Ivy, her father could be a mean old sod. An incident that springs to mind to demonstrate his meanness occurred not long after we started courting. We were all sitting in the lounge one day, when Ivy told her husband to get me a drink, by the look on his face you'd have thought she'd told him to give me his life savings. He begrudgingly got up from his armchair, huffed and puffed as he opened a sideboard door and retrieved an ancient looking bottle of cheap VP wine. He poured me about a thimbleful and swigged the rest straight from the bottle. Having said that, I think I was grateful for his meanness, as the wine was as cheap and nasty as you can get. As well as being a tight fisted sod, he was as crafty as they come, working as a painter during the summer while the weather was fine, but as soon as it began to get colder he'd pack in the outdoor work, managing to wangle a job inside as a boilerman!

At that time I was getting hold of some decent clothing, which I either sold off or traded for other items. Amongst these trades, I had managed to swap some items for Whisky and cigarettes. When I was at Wendy's house one day, I presented Ivy with some clothes and cigarettes and her husband with a quart bottle of the Whisky, which had come from the American PX stores on military bases. The PX stores were intended to supply duty free goods for the American Servicemen's own personal use, but there were always opportunities for a bit of bartering with the Yanks. A huge grin came over his face as he grabbed the bottle, once again he begrudgingly asked me if I'd like a nip. I've never liked Whisky, still don't and told him so. This pleased him even more, he wouldn't have to share it with anyone, the mean old git. He set about devouring the bottle and was starting his third glass as we left for our evening out. Wendy also met my parents as our relationship progressed and we became quite an item. Mum liked Wendy and in no time at all they were getting along famously. Dad was another matter, he'd never been the most sociable of people and didn't show his feelings that much. I presumed he liked Wendy, he didn't say anything negative at least. She was really my first serious girlfriend and all went well, however Wendy's father was getting upset at the time of night that she was getting back home after our dates. He reprimanded her many times with vague threats of throwing her out. I don't think Wendy thought for one moment he was really serious and would follow this threat through. However, he was and one night as I dropped her off home, he was waiting for us and let us know in no uncertain terms that enough was enough. I apologised profusely and tried to tell him that it was my fault and that I had kept Wendy out late even though she wanted to come home. He wouldn't listen and dragged her inside. I met Wendy from work the next day and she told me her father had given her a week to get out. The poor girl was distraught and at a loss as to what to do. I calmed her down and told her I'd sort something out. There was no way my parents would allow her to stay at our family home. At that time, such arrangements were almost unheard of. We'd have been the talk of the neighbourhood.

I had to do something and fast. Now knowing what a miserable, tight-fisted old sod her father was, I was in no doubt that when the week was up, she'd be out, whether she had somewhere to go or not. He probably reasoned he'd be better off financially. The very next day I managed to secure a large room at a reasonable rent just off the Edgware Road at Colindale.

I arranged to pick Wendy up from her parent's place and help her move her belongings. When I arrived I could see she was upset, however she managed a big smile for me and gave me a big hug. Ivy came out of the front room as we were shifting her stuff into the car, it was obvious from the look on her face, that Wendy's eviction from the family home was not of her doing. It was all down to her father. He didn't show his face once during this time, which was probably just as well. I think I may have been inclined to give him a piece of my mind, or more. When Wendy's belongings were finally packed in the car, she said her goodbyes to her Mum. Poor Ivy couldn't hide her tears, neither could Wendy come to that, but I felt encouraged when Ivy told me that even though she was sorry to see her daughter leaving home, she was reassured, as she was certain I'd take good care of Wendy. I had always liked Ivy and her saying that really meant a lot to me. It made me feel good about myself, just a few words from a nice lady like Ivy had made all the difference. It had turned an initially, very upsetting situation into a real positive. Wendy was obviously upset at having to leave her Mum and her two sisters, Brenda and Susan behind. However I think she realised that it was going to happen sooner or later and now that it had, there was much to look forward to. As we drove to Wendy's new lodgings, I looked across at her, this pretty little girl smiling back at me and realised how much she actually meant to me. Whether it was her being thrown out and the new situation this brought on that made me realise it, I don't know, but I was certain now....I was in love.

It didn't take her long to settle into her new room and she soon made it a real home. It was very close to where I was living with my parents and I made sure she didn't feel too alone by visiting her on a daily basis. I was either at her place or she was at mine. My Mum and younger brother Bob liked Wendy and they were always happy to be in her company, even Dad had come around somewhat! He actually managed the odd bit of conversation now and again, which for him was a rarity. She was always included in our family days out. On a Sunday we'd regularly have a drive out to the coast or sometimes a motorboat trip on the Thames at Henley, Wendy always enjoyed them immensely.

Wendy obviously kept in touch with her family, as she missed her Mum and sisters and, to a certain extent, her father as well. I'd take her round to her parents place and Ivy would always make me very welcome. The old man would just sit in his armchair and grunt. On one occasion, Ivy mentioned that she overheard a conversation between her husband and one of his pals, who had enquired about Wendy, during which he said "No, I slung her out and she went off with "Old Sticky Fingers".

Strange how he didn't seem to mind 'Old Sticky Fingers' when I was handing him cigarettes and quart bottles of Whisky, the hypocritical old git!

After a while, it just seemed the most natural progression to our relationship to get married. I proposed to Wendy, she said yes and that was that. We didn't make a big thing of it, I think we both knew it was on the cards to happen sooner or later. Wendy was pleased, as even though she loved her little room and I was with her a great deal, I felt she still got lonely on her own sometimes. We eagerly looked forward to being together.

Even though I didn't particularly like or respect Wendy's father, I still thought it would be proper to seek his permission to marry his daughter, so off I went. Wendy wanted to come, but this was something I felt I should do alone. I arrived and Ivy answered the door. She was pleased to see me but looked surprised that I was alone. I told her why I was there and she gave me a hug, telling me how delighted she was. Her husband was in the front room and I was shown in, Ivy leaving me to it. I told old misery guts that I was planning on marrying Wendy and that I'd love his approval. Having got to know the type of man he was, it was probably foolish of me, but somehow I expected him to come around a bit, maybe even congratulate me, but no, not in the slightest. He looked at me and said,

" Do you know what you're doing? She's a right lazy cow, she'll make a terrible wife".

As much as I wanted to give him a clump, I bit my tongue, ignored his comment and asked his permission.

"Do what you like" was the reply.

I shook my head in disbelief and left the room. As Ivy showed me out, I told her that her husband had given his permission and didn't elaborate any further. I'm sure she already knew what type of man he was and didn't need me to upset her any further.

The arrangements were made and we married in the summer of 1961 at Harrow Registry office, for which I had to pay the grand sum of 7/6d (37 1/2p). It was only a small wedding, my parents attended and were pleased for me, as they thought a lot of Wendy (even Dad). Old misery guts (Wendy's father) didn't attend, which was no big surprise to me, knowing how unsociable he was, but Wendy was upset. You would think that any father would be pleased to attend his daughter's wedding, maybe he thought he'd have to treat all the guests to a drink in the pub afterwards. However, Ivy came and shed a few tears, she really was a lovely lady. She still called me 'Thingy' though! We all went to the pub and had a few drinks after the ceremony and had a nice time. The following day, Ivy laid on a bit of a do at her place. I think she was a bit embarrassed that her husband had been absent for the wedding. The old man made a bit of an effort and at least pretended he was pleased, even if he wasn't. However, I'm sure I actually saw a bit of a smile for a split second.

CHAPTER FOUR
MARRIED LIFE

Obviously, we now wanted our own place and after a bit of searching, I had soon acquired the tenancy of a rented flat in Honeypot Lane, Stanmore, for which I paid a local tradesman £200 key money, a fair amount of cash in those days. It was a lovely little, self-contained place and we soon made it our home.

I was still working in the building trade, bringing home decent money most of the time, however, villainy was still very much part of my life. Wendy wasn't really too aware of that side of my life prior to our marriage, as we had never lived together, so I'd managed to keep her blissfully unaware.

I think she may have suspected I wasn't totally straight though, as I supplied the majority of the new furniture for our marital home by robbing a show home on a newly built estate nearby! It was inevitable though, that now we were living as man and wife she would soon find out. When she did first realise what I was about, it was certainly a case of 'in for a penny, in for a pound'. I came home one day carrying a large carrier bag and Wendy enquired whether I had been shopping. I emptied the contents of the bag onto the dining table and she let out a loud gasp. The bag contained £3400 in masses of mixed denomination notes. In 1962 this was a considerable sum of money, enough to buy a small house, however only half was mine. My partner in crime at that time, Ron, was due 50%, but didn't want to take his share back home just yet, as he was still living with his parents.

When Wendy finally managed to lift her chin from her chest after the shock, she obviously asked where the money came from. I explained that we had broken into a local business' premises and stolen it. Being totally unaccustomed to situations like this, she told me to take it back. I think she came out with a daft comment like, "you'll get in trouble". I told her that we knew for a fact the money had been left in cash at the business, as it was totally undeclared for tax avoidance reasons and that the theft would probably go unreported. She seemed unconvinced and looked as though she was about to panic. I sat her down and made her a cup of tea, in an attempt to calm her down. She looked slightly more composed, so I went to take a bath, having got myself grubby from the break-in. When I came back into the front room wrapped in a towel, Wendy was sat at the table with the money sorted out into various separate piles.

"What's all this?" I asked.

Pointing to them one after the other, she said "this one's for a new sofa, this one's for a holiday, this one's for new carpets, this one's for that coat I saw last week" and so on.

It seemed that given a few minutes on her own with the cash had initiated a total change of heart for her. I think this is a prime example of how money can totally corrupt. Wendy was (up until that moment) a completely straight, honest young lady, but having a large sum of cash stuck in front of her, changed her outlook somewhat. Needless to say the cash came in very handy at that time as we were still getting our home together and Wendy had also recently discovered she was pregnant. The money helped to finance all the necessities for our eagerly anticipated arrival and on the 14th January 1962, our first born child, Jane was born and she was beautiful. We were both delighted, we were now a proper family, not that it made me any more responsible. My brother introduced me to a friend of his, Tony, a secondhand furniture dealer who specialised in house clearances, who had a beautiful Dynatron Safari record player for sale. Knowing that I had cash around me at that time and that I was still in the process of furnishing my house, he thought I may well be interested.

I showed it to Wendy and as this particular model of record player was very much the 'in thing' at the time, she fell in love with it. I paid him £25 and he assured me that there was absolutely no comeback on it at all. After this deal I began to see a lot more of Tony and he came round one day to see if I'd be interested in joining him on a job. He knew of a major rag trade dealer, who lived at Golder's Green and apparently, he regularly parked his vehicle outside his house at night, fully loaded with dresses, coats and suits etc. Sounding a good earner, I agreed immediately and we arranged to go the following night. Tony came round to my place the next night as arranged and we set off in my car. We arrived at the merchant's beautiful house, situated in a very nice road. This looked promising, the dealer was obviously doing very well for himself if he lived in this style. Unfortunately, his gown van was nowhere to be seen. We thought maybe he'd parked it elsewhere, out of the way of villains like us, so we checked in neighbouring streets but to no avail. Having made the effort to come out at this time of night, we were reluctant to go home empty handed, so began to look for any other potential opportunities. As luck would have it, we discovered a van loaded with cigarettes. We hotwired this van (much, much easier in those days) and drove it off.

In a quiet nearby road we unloaded as many of the best quality cigarettes, as would fit into my car and drove back to my flat in Stanmore. Being around 3 a.m., Wendy was fast asleep. I began to unload the cigarettes upstairs into a wardrobe, while Tony stayed downstairs. Later that night, around 4am, the Police raided the flat. They obviously found the cigarettes and seemed to know where they came from and how we obtained them.

I learnt much later on, that Tony had informed the Police. Unbeknown to me, he was a heroin addict and was wanted on many more serious offences linked, or as a result of his addiction. He had initiated a deal with the Police, where in return for grassing me, (the Police were desperate to get me behind bars at that time) Tony would be excused various other offences. As a result, on 25th July 1962, at Hampstead Magistrates Court I received my first custodial sentence of three months imprisonment for theft, to run concurrent with one months imprisonment for taking a motor vehicle without consent and another month concurrent for no insurance. A twelve month driving ban was thrown in for good measure as well. Tony received the same sentence and after a long wait in the cells below the court, we were both sent off to Brixton prison to serve our time. At this time I was unaware of Tony putting me in the frame, this came to light later on. It hadn't taken more than a year of married life to give poor Wendy a taste of what life was like being married to a career criminal.

CHAPTER FIVE
A FIRST TASTE OF PORRIDGE

When I think back now, it seems an absolute miracle that I managed to reach the age of 24 before being banged up. The amount of skulduggery I'd been involved in from such a young age was to such an extent, I had escaped justice with nothing else but sheer luck. However, my good fortune had finally run out and it was certainly a rude awakening.

I can remember the feeling of dread as I was shut into the cubicle of the Black Maria meat wagon for the drive from court to Brixton. Tony was in the neighbouring box, not that we spoke on the journey, I wasn't in the mood. Tony was probably elated though, a three month sentence for him was getting away lightly, not that I knew that then. The wagon finally pulled into the intimidating gates of the prison and we were taken out of our sweaty boxes and herded through into reception.

Prisons, by their nature, are not what you could describe as welcoming and back in the early 60's, Brixton was certainly nearing the top of the 'unwelcoming' league. I have been back there recently, (on a voluntary basis!) and though hardly luxurious, conditions are much improved, but in 1962 it was an absolute filth pit. The stench of urine and sweat as you entered was overpowering, enough to make me gag, much to the amusement of the guards.

On entering reception, the guard completed the necessary paperwork and we were told to strip and surrender our clothes in readiness for prison uniform. Also, we would be given a medical examination by the Prison Doctor. Tony and I stripped off and he looked embarrassed enough to cover his privates with his hands.

The doctor shouted "let's have a look at you son, you haven't got anything I've not seen before!".

Tony reluctantly and slowly removed his hands from his groin, to reveal a large wrap of sticking plaster around the end of his penis.

"What the hell is that" screamed the doctor.

The screws couldn't contain their laughter and to be honest, neither could I.

Tony, who by this time was a shade of crimson I'd rarely seen, explained, "my bird doesn't trust me with other women, so she puts this round my cock and draws a cross over the join, so I can't get at it with anyone else".

The place was in uproar, everyone was crying with laughter and it somehow lightened a difficult time. The doctor obviously ordered him to remove it, which was funnier still, I can still hear the noises he made as the VERY sticky plaster was removed from an extremely delicate area!

We were issued with our uniforms, which consisted of an army style flannel tunic jacket and trousers, heavy boots, a thick canvas shirt, woollen socks and an enormous pair of underpants. The whole kit absolutely stunk, god knows how many men had worn it before me, but judging by the smell and the appearance of the underpants I'd say the number ran well into treble figures. This disgusted me, I was totally unprepared for this. I don't really know what I expected, maybe I should have realised we wouldn't be issued with a silk dressing gown and slippers and that a prison sentence was meant to be a punishment. As strange as it seems, considering the way my life and criminal career had been progressing, I'd not really considered going to prison as a possibility. This was totally naive of me and this sentence came as an almighty reality check. After dressing in this dreadful and pathetic looking uniform, I shuffled along following the prison officer to my cell. I say 'shuffled', as even after answering the question "what size boots?" with "a nine, guv", I was issued with a very large eleven!

After a long stressful day, I was glad to get into my bunk, (stinking as it was) in an effort to shut it all out. I barely acknowledged my two cell mates laying on their bunks, I was that exhausted. I fell asleep almost immediately.

I was awoken early the next morning by the disgusting sound of someone clearing their throat. I opened my eyes just in time to see a massive lump of phlegm fly past my bunk and thump onto the floor alongside me. (If you're eating your dinner while reading this, I apologise!) I remonstrated with the animal in the upper bunk and threatened him with a clump if he dared do that again. Just as I calmed down, another old lag came back through the now open door of the cell carrying a bowl of porridge. He promptly pulled out his pot, dropped his trousers and pants, sat down and started to go to the toilet while eating his breakfast!

"What the fuck are you doing?", I screamed.

"I always have a shit while I'm eating my porridge", he replied.

"Not while I'm here you don't" and once again made a threat of violence to stop this idiot.

What a welcoming! My first day inside and they'd put me in a cell with two farmyard animals. I have always been pretty fastidious regarding tidiness and personal hygiene, so I wasn't about to change now, even with the limitations of being incarcerated. I went for my breakfast and had a word with a prison officer. I explained the situation to him, he was hardly sympathetic but give him some credit, managed to get me a move to another cell relatively quickly. My two new cell mates were at least human in their habits.

Looking back now, over my many prison sentences, I think this 3 month stint in Brixton was the worst of the lot. I realise this sounds ridiculous, considering what was to happen later in my life, but I really do think this was the case. It was an absolute hell-hole and the sentence was a 3 month long nightmare. This wasn't helped by the time of year, the summer of 1962 must have been a scorcher as I vividly remember sweating like a stuck-pig throughout my entire time there. It was like living in a sauna. Also, the food was as close to inedible as I've witnessed. Almost everyday our main meal was described as 'goulash', what was in this 'goulash' I hate to think. I'm pretty sure that each day's leftovers were served up the next day...and the next day, topped up with any old crap that was hanging around in the kitchen. However, it was a 'take it or leave it' situation and I didn't fancy finishing my sentence as a bag of bones, so I shovelled it down, albeit very reluctantly.

Many, many times in Brixton, I recall thinking to myself, never again. If only I'd taken notice of my thoughts, what path would my life had taken. Also, considering how bad a time I had during this sentence, WHY didn't I take any notice of my thoughts? I'm sure the psychologists amongst you could offer many theories on this and believe me, I've probably considered every possible reason for the way my life turned out. However, the truthful answer is I just don't know.

I saw my wife Wendy only once during my time in Brixton, when my brother Peter brought her in. She looked totally shell-shocked sat there in the visiting room. Our daughter Jane was little more than six months old and poor Wendy was feeling the strain without me being around to help. Also, she found out during my time in Brixton that she was pregnant with our second child. Try as I might to lighten her mood during the visit, she was having none of it. Conversation was difficult and to be honest, it was a relief when the visit was over. Long awkward silences seem even longer on a prison visit, so it was probably just as well this was her only time.

CHAPTER SIX
BACK GRAFTING

The three months of hell finally ended and as I came out through the gates, I saw the comforting sight of my brother Peter sat in his car waiting to pick me up. He drove me back to my flat and Wendy was waiting there. It felt so good to be back home in comfortable surroundings, after the horrors of Brixton. I spent the next few days re-aquatinting myself with my wife and my surroundings.

Maybe I should have used this time to reassess where my life was heading, as Jane was now ten months old and Wendy was four months into her pregnancy with our second. Unfortunately I didn't and once again I don't really have any explanation why. Brixton had really had an effect on me, but why didn't it have enough effect to turn my life away from crime? I have racked my brain for hours on this over the years, but to no avail.

Was I just a born villain? Did I have no real control over my actions? This would be a handy excuse for me to use, unfortunately I don't believe a word of it. I think a more plausible explanation would be my upbringing previously mentioned. Perhaps if my parents had been perfectly 'straight', my life would have taken a different course, who knows? It's all immaterial now anyway.

Some months after finishing my sentence in Brixton, I finally found out the full score concerning Tony getting me put away in Brixton, I'd had a feeling in the back of my mind that something wasn't quite right about the whole thing, but had dismissed it. As strange as it may sound now, I think maybe I was a little naive and too trusting. Needless to say, I ended all association with Tony as soon as my fears concerning him were proved. My discovery about him also cost me financially.

Having settled back into home life, I was soon looking for money. Three months away had eaten into the family finances severely and I had not managed to find any work in the building trade. Further strains on my wallet came in March of that year, (1963) when our son David was born. It was utter madness, me carrying on with my criminal activities in my situation, but I had my head down on a mission to get money as quick as I could, no matter what.

I had met an old pal one afternoon, while looking at cars at a local dealers. We hadn't seen one another since our school days and we renewed our friendship over a coffee in a local cafe. It transpired that my friend was a real scallywag and had three children by three different women and that he led totally separate lives with all of them. He worked, like myself, in the building trade and managed somehow to juggle his rather complicated life around by telling a cock and bull story about having to go away to work to two of these poor women while staying with the other and so on. How he managed it, I've no idea. He must have had the best memory in the world, I think the stress of the situation would have done for me! Anyway, his lifestyle was crippling him financially and on hearing I'd just got out of the nick recently, he put a proposition to me. He knew of a large chemist's shop which had a very well stocked pharmacy department that would be easy to break into. I remembered that Tony had mentioned some time ago, that if I ever managed to get hold of any drugs, he would take the lot from me. With this in mind, I agreed to help my friend on the job.

All went according to plan and without problems. We managed to break in easily enough and came away with quite a decent haul, including a stash of drugs from the locked cabinet, i.e. Opiates etc. I had explained the arrangement with Tony to myfriend and he was happy to go along. We met Tony and handed the drugs over, with him promising that as soon as they were sold, we'd see some cash.

A week or two passed by with no word from Tony. I finally managed to contact him and he fed me some story about the Police having arrested him and confiscated the drugs.

Alarm bells now started to ring, but as much as I didn't believe him, I couldn't prove otherwise. This made me look a total fool to my friend I'd done the job with. I retold this story to my brother shortly afterwards and as I mentioned in an earlier chapter, he told me that Tony was a heroin addict, this more or less confirmed my suspicions.

I also discovered the truth about him doing the deal re. the Brixton sentence. I had learnt my lesson the hard way. I was certainly less likely to take people on face value from then on.

Some months after coming out of Brixton I met a thief named Frank. I was reliably informed that he was the man to know, as he had been one of the best 'Peter Men' (safe blowers) around. We soon became friends and he took me under his wing as far as learning the fine art of blowing open safes. Coming from an engineering background certainly helped in learning the safe blowing game. Frank was meticulous in his working habits, some might say a real 'craftsman' and he seemed to get great pleasure and almost pride, in passing on his considerable knowledge. Many 'Petermen' at this time were making the mistake of using far too much explosives in trying to enter the safe and there were some terrible incidents of men being maimed or even killed by this costly error. The art was to use the absolute minimum of explosives required to do the job. This involved in blowing JUST the lock of the safe, (rather than attempting to blow the door off) and then using tools to finish the job.

I worked with Frank for a while, but had aspirations of working solo. Through underworld connections I was put in contact with John, known as 'J.A.'. We arranged to meet in a pub in Wembley and I explained what I had in mind. After a couple of beers we went out to his motor in the car park and he produced a stick of gelignite for me that he wanted twenty quid for. However, he suggested that we work together and even though I eventually wanted to work alone, such was his reputation, I was keen to work with him for the time being.

Our first job together wasn't the big pay-off we were hoping for though. We had been given information concerning a safe in an office by some railway sidings where coal was stored and traded. After breaking in and blowing the safe, which took some effort we found the princely sum of 1s 4d in pennies and a handwritten note asking 'Fred' to use the money to buy the cat some food. It was not what we expected, but anyway...the cat went hungry and we were richer to the extent of 8d each! We also learnt a valuable lesson, in that not all information is good information. I was basically 'up' for anything at this time, I was desperate to get some money behind me, to have some sense of security. I knew from past experience how having a bit tucked away took the pressure off and desperately wanted to feel that sense of security again.

So when I was approached by a man with a proposition which potentially would net me and JA a tidy sum, I had no hesitation in jumping at it. Apparently there was a high street business premises, which had a safe containing the money, however the safe was in the front of this shop, in full view from the street. Therefore, we'd have to turn the safe around so we could work in the darkness at the rear of the store and then when we'd finished, turn the safe back around to ensure the robbery would not be discovered until the next day.

We got into the premises from the back entrance without problem, swivelled the large safe around, blew the lock and netted the contents. Unfortunately, yet again, it was nowhere near what we had expected but still a decent night's work. We later discovered that the guy who'd fed us the information was in cahoots with the businessman who owned the store and that they had split the majority of the cash between themselves and the owner claimed the cash in his insurance claim. We had put ourselves at risk for far, far less than they pocketed and they had no real chance of getting nicked. They had used us and we fell for it.

Another job that didn't go quite to plan around this time was put to us by a club owner, who knew he was being fiddled out of a fortune by his business partner. The partner was the accountant, who was using clever practices to divert much of their takings his way. The club owner knew this was going on, but was unable to prove it.

He was pretty sure the funds from his partner's clever bookkeeping were being held in a safe, in cash. He had a good idea where this safe was and on the promise of a decent whack, we'd attempt to get back what was rightly his.

Without saying too much, we managed to get to the safe and were making good progress, but were interrupted midway through the job. So we made a quick getaway, only managing to take one of many large sacks of sixpenny pieces which were sat along the side of the safe. These were, presumably, the takings from the one-arm bandits in the clubs. The coins totalled exactly 100 pounds, not quite what we were hoping for! Failed jobs like these were happening a bit too often for JA and myself and to rub salt into the wound, we later found out that inside the safe that we were so close to getting into, was close on 50,000 pounds, no small sum now, but an absolute fortune back then!

In between occasional building, decorating jobs and the attempted bits of villainy, I had managed to secure a market pitch in Chapel Street, Islington, a busy street market to this day. I was in partnership with another chap which worked well for me, as when other work arose for me, the stall remained manned. It was regular money when things weren't going to plan on other fronts. We sold ladies handbags, always a good mover, which I had learned from experience..."a lady can't have too many handbags", my wife used to say to me!

I had rented a lock-up garage from a nice lady for a few quid a week, which was at the end of her garden. She knew I was a builder and to all intents and purposes was using the garage to store building materials and my tools, as well as my stock for the market stall. This was partly true, however, it was also perfect for storing any knocked off gear which came my way, as well as my tools and materials for my safe-breaking activities (gelignite). I made sure the garage door was safe and secure by replacing the cheap, flimsy lock with two heavy duty padlocks. I couldn't afford to have anyone getting in there, for obvious reasons. Things also improved on the villainy side when we realised the potential of stealing cigarettes. Tobacconist's shops became a favourite hunting ground for us, cigarettes have always been easy to move on and cartons of 200 are relatively small in size, so large numbers can be stolen and transported in the boot of a car. The lock-up garage was perfect for storing stashes of cigarettes prior to selling them on. At first we sold to friends and family members, but a carton at a time made it a slow business getting rid of the stock. However we managed to come to a very useful agreement with a fence in Willesden, named Bill.

Whatever we had, Bill would take from us and pay cash on the nail. This suited us perfectly, a quick turnaround, the stock was off loaded almost immediately, ensuring they weren't in our possession too long. Our luck had changed at last!

I had managed to thieve a load of canvas mailbags, which were perfect for loading the cigarettes into when on the job in the shops and taking over to Bill. I can recall a funny incident concerning Bill and the cigarettes; J.A. and I had thieved a large load of Players and Capstan cigarettes, which Bill favoured at that time, (apparently they were his best sellers), and we drove them round to his house one evening, leaving it quite late, ensuring we had a bit of cover from darkness of night. Bill let us in and we dragged the bags of cigarettes upstairs. We worked out a price for the load and Bill paid us out, then asked us to sling the bags into his spare room along the corridor. I dragged several bags to the next door along, opened the door and threw several sacks onto the bed. As soon as they landed, a large piercing scream broke the silence. Bill came rushing out just as a body sat up in the bed, sending the bags onto the floor. I'd gone into the wrong room, this was the marital bedroom and Bill's missus was the poor soul who'd had several thousand cigarettes dumped on her. She wasn't best pleased I can tell you and J.A. and myself made a quick exit, just managing to let Bill know we'd be in touch again soon. Whether he managed to hear us over the tirade of abuse being thrown at him by his wife, I'm not sure.

At that time, I had money coming in from all directions and the experience of my previous incarceration was long forgotten, or at least put to the back of my mind. Thieving was in my blood and it was more or less inevitable I would be back 'at it' sooner or later.

Due to having a bit more cash than usual, I had managed to save some cash and was was looking to purchase a house in Kenton. It was currently divided into two flats but would be a lovely, large family home once converted back into a single dwelling. I had paid five hundred pounds deposit, towards the purchase price of five thousand five hundred pounds. I got some strange looks when I paid this deposit in tenners and fivers, but explained that I was a builder and my invoices were often settled in cash! A mortgage was arranged for the balance and I took possession of the keys and made a start on the conversion, knocking out and bricking up several fireplaces, as was the fashion at the time (nowadays people love the old-style fireplaces).

During this period, we were contacted by an underworld acquaintance who had lined us up to rob a lorry that was due to pass through a fairly deserted stretch of road in Epping Forest. This lorry would be carrying an extremely large load of good quality whiskey. The driver of the truck was in on the job, so there would be no resistance. Thinking this job was as good as done, we started to take many orders for the whiskey from pub and club proprietors we knew and all was looking good. The date and time was arranged and JA and myself drove out to the arranged spot in Epping. The designated time came, no lorry...we thought maybe he'd been held up by traffic, so we sat and waited. After two hours, we decided enough was enough and aborted the job. Two men, both with criminal records, sat in a car in the middle of the night in Epping Forest would prove difficult to explain, should local Police come looking!

Now we were in a bit of a situation, we had taken enough orders to clear a large percentage of what we were anticipating nabbing on this job and rather than lose face and reputation by letting these people down, we needed a large quantity of whiskey...and fast. A few days later, while driving through Wembley, I'd noticed a large Victoria Wine Company shop. I parked up to take a closer look and lo and behold, the flat above the shop was empty. Later that night JA and myself broke into the flat, which was easy enough, as a Yale lock was all the security in place. We pulled up the floorboards and cut a hole in the ceiling, just large enough through which to climb into the store below.

Once inside, we emptied the shop, taking everything through the backdoor entrance into a van we had parked behind the store. We were away in no time at all, pleased with our night's work and drove the van back to my new place in Kenton with the idea of parking up on the driveway and unloading the loot into the empty property, the idea being that I wasn't yet known to anyone in this area, including the Police. However when we arrived, someone had parked over the entrance to my driveway and I was unable to gain access. I had no option but to drive back to my flat and park the van up there, ready to start serving our pre-arranged customers the next day.

JA arrived at my place early next morning, ready to join me on our drop-offs. Unbeknown to us, one of our potential clients, unhappy with the price we were asking at the pre-order stage had grassed us up and the Police were ready and waiting for us. I'd seen J.A. arrive in his Dormobile and had gone out to meet him. I went over to the van containing the spirits and it wouldn't start. While trying to fire it up, I noticed two coppers approaching JA's vehicle. Realising they were onto us, I jumped from the van and ran off into an alley. JA had just managed to get away as well, even after one of the coppers opening the door of JA's motor and throwing a truncheon in his direction, which fortunately missed, leaving a sizeable dent in the bodywork! We were now on the run, the Police would now have the stolen goods in their possession and us without a leg to stand on.

We didn't manage to evade capture for long though, as a vehicle we were using on other jobs was a 'ringer' (stolen vehicle 'rung' to a differing identity) and had been reported to the Police, as we'd left it parked awkwardly. They'd arrived to check it out, discovered the discrepancy in the vehicle's number plates and chassis number and lay in wait. As we arrived to pick the vehicle up, I was coshed across the head and awoke in a Police Station, having the gash made by the truncheon stitched up.

I was charged with various offences, which included the breaking and entering at the Victoria Wine Company and also, the stolen vehicle charges etc. I appeared at the County of Middlesex Sessions in November of 1963, where I was sentenced to 2 years and 3 months imprisonment and also a 4 year driving disqualification.

After a short cool down in the court's cells, I was shut (once again) into one of the claustrophobic little cubicles of the 'Black Maria' and driven the (thankfully) relatively short journey to Wormwood Scrubs in west London.

CHAPTER SEVEN
THE SCRUBS

The 'Scrubs', (as most older prisons are), is an intimidating looking place and as I looked out of the tiny window as we pulled up to the gate, I had a terrible sick feeling in my stomach. Deservedly so, I hear you say and I agree, prisons are there for a purpose and that is to persuade inmates to avoid further spells inside, not that it had that effect on me. After my horrible time in Brixton less than a year ago, what was I doing going back inside? Once again, without meaning to sound repetitive, I really can't answer. Maybe I had just grown to accept prison as an occupational hazard, an unpleasant but inevitable interruption to an exciting lifestyle that occurred occasionally. I enjoyed the buzz that crime, particularly thieving gave me, maybe that had become a sort of addiction. I know that if I hadn't been 'at it' for a while, I missed the thrill and excitement it gave me, often the thrill of the job was more satisfying than any financial reward.

Whatever the reason, Wormwood Scrubs was to be home for the duration of my sentence. To make matters worse, obviously the house purchase had been scrapped and I only received a small portion of the 500 pound deposit back due to 'damage' to the property (the removal of the fireplaces).

Fortunately, Wormwood Scrubs was within easy reach of my family home, enabling my wife to visit regularly, but once again I had put poor Wendy under so much pressure. She was left alone to cope with two very young children on her own. Also, ONCE AGAIN she found out she was pregnant with our third child shortly after I was sentenced and during my time there, our third child Lucy was born in June 1964. Looking back, I'm amazed how poor Wendy kept it all together, but she did and managed an amazingly good job of it for which I am eternally grateful.

I settled down, as best I could, to accepting the time I was to be there, hoping to serve my sentence with as little fuss and stress as possible. Unfortunately, this didn't prove to be possible:- I had started weightlifting shortly after being put into the 'Scrubs' as I intended to stay as fit as I could, (having always been keen to look after myself) and took to the sport like a duck to water. I was in C Wing and our team were in strict training for an inter-wing competition with D Wing, which housed the lifers. Training was going well until I began to feel unwell, I dismissed it and trained on, hoping it would pass. However, I felt increasingly rough as time went on. I was experiencing severe chest pains and was noticing dramatic weight loss. I was now beginning to worry and decided to see the Prison Doctor. He checked me over and sent me packing, telling me that he thought I was malingering.

My condition deteriorated further and I requested another consultation. This also proved useless in getting a proper diagnosis, other than being prescribed the universal prison remedy of a foul smelling and tasting concoction, we called 'onion water'. They made you drink this muck in front of them, if you didn't you were reported for refusing treatment. Christ knows what was in this concoction, or what it was meant to do, but it had no benefit to me whatsoever and my condition worsened. I saw the same doctor time and time again over a period of several months, but to no avail, he continued to insist I was pulling a fast one. My weight had dropped from around 12 stone down to 9 stone 7lbs and I insisted on being checked over more thoroughly. I managed this by ringing constantly on my bell in the middle of the night and screaming in agony, until the screws finally took me to the prison hospital. I was admitted and spent the night there. The following morning, this same moronic doctor came to see me, insisted I was still malingering and ordered me to be put into a strip cell with a bread and water diet for three days to 'sort me out'.

Now this cell was in the confines of the prison hospital wing and if you spend more than 24 hours in the hospital, a chest x-ray is compulsory. The x-ray was taken and I was then placed into a comfortable single cell for a while, before being x-rayed again. After this, I was taken to a proper single bed hospital ward and as I entered, I had noticed signs on the door, informing any person entering to wear a mask and protective clothing. Now I was worried. I knew all along I was ill and seeing this more or less confirmed my fears.

After a worrying hour or so, my 'not so favourite' doctor came in and calmly informed me that I had TB. I really tore into him, calling him all the names under the sun. I told him in no uncertain terms that he wasn't fit to be a vet let alone a doctor.

He was livid, stamping around screaming "how dare you speak to me like that", but I was in no mood to back down.

I now had a life threatening illness, which had probably been present and undiagnosed for months and this idiot had been feeding me nothing but this 'onion water' and telling me that I was trying to pull a fast one. Anyhow, I was taken and admitted to a civilian hospital close to the Scrubs. After endless tests, I was informed that I had been very fortunate in that even though the TB had not been recognised by this idiot, I was in fact over the worst of it and it was already on the mend. I recuperated in the hospital until I was fit enough to return to the prison.

To my knowledge, no action was taken against this doctor. I often wonder whether he would have got off so lightly, had my condition worsened after the TB diagnosis. However it probably wouldn't have made any difference, I imagine they would have bent the facts to suit the doctor rather than me.

Fortunately, after this the remainder of my sentence passed without any further major incident, in fact for the last few months of my sentence I was being taken out on a daily basis by a civilian Trades Assistant on little decorating jobs etc, mainly in Prison Officer's house. I was released just over a year later in June of 1965 after serving 18 months.

I returned home to Wendy and my three kids and it suddenly dawned on me how much of their early lives I'd already missed. Jane was now almost 3 1/2 years old, David a little over two and little Lucy just a year and since Jane's birth I had spent 21 months of that time in prison. Effectively, Jane was the only one of our children that I had spent any time with.

With this in mind I threw myself into making up for lost time and spent every moment I could with the kids and my lovely wife. I know Wendy had been through a rough time, what with our three children coming along in such a short period and me being locked up for a considerable section of that time. I was determined to make it up to her, or rather I THOUGHT I was determined. However, we were very much in love and I owed her so much for putting up with my lifestyle. I hadn't been there when she really needed me, but she was fortunate to have had the support of some very good and dear friends.

During this period, we spent some lovely times together, driving out to the coast or the countryside on Sundays and within a short period of time, I felt settled. The kids had begun to get to know me, as when I first got out I could sense an obvious wariness in their attitude to me, which of course I understood. All three were still babies and suddenly this man, little more than a stranger comes onto their lives from nowhere, but this soon passed and I became their Dad once more.

I hadn't seen anything of my brothers, Peter and Bob while I was in the Scrubs, so tried to arrange to meet and catch up with them. I met Peter first and we spent a day together. As mentioned earlier, Peter had led a somewhat dubious life and had been in a bit of trouble himself, but was managing to keep himself fairly straight at that time.

My younger brother Bob, was very different to myself and Pete and had never really been attracted to criminal activities in the way we were. However, he had got into smoking marijuana in a big way and was mixing with a crowd with very much the same interests. I discovered this when I visited his house a few days after my day with Peter.

I went to his house in Notting Hill and was told by his wife that he was visiting friends who lived locally. She gave me the address, it wasn't too far away so I made my way round there. The door was answered by a pretty American girl and after telling her I was there to see Bob, she showed me into a room where my brother was sat on the floor with about eight other people. A thick fug of sweet smelling smoke hovered above them as they greeted me, after being introduced by Bob. We exchanged pleasantries and they invited me to sit down and join them. As I did, one of the crowd started to roll a joint. It was sparked up and passed around until it was offered to me. I wasn't even a regular smoker of tobacco and at that stage had never smoked dope, but encouraged by my brother, started to puff away at the joint. Being totally naive as to the etiquette of joint smoking, rather than taking a few drags and passing it on, I smoked the whole thing! I could see them all giggling at my lack of knowledge of the rules of dope smoking, however it wasn't until I'd put out the joint stub that they informed me where I'd gone wrong. By this time the drug was taking effect and I was beginning to start a cold sweat and began to worry what was happening to me. I decided fresh air was my best bet and told Bob I was leaving. I made to stand up, but my legs wouldn't seem to do what my brain was asking them! Paranoia started to set in and I began to panic.

"Aaah" I screamed, "what's happened to my legs? They won't work!"

The room erupted into laughter and this made me worse. I was still struggling to get to my feet while my brother and his friends fell around the floor, almost wetting themselves at my distress. Eventually, Bob told me to sit down and breathe slowly and that the feeling will soon pass. I followed his instructions and sure enough, I soon began to feel somewhat better. As soon as my legs began to work again, I left them to it and made my way out into the fresh air of the street. That was the first and last time I smoked drugs for a good few years!

I had managed to get back into work in the building trade and for a while, things ticked over nicely, that is until I began to see J.A. again regularly. I'm not trying to blame him for my early return to crime, far from it, in most cases it was me who instigated it. I was a compulsive thief who loved the buzz that crime gave me. A brief period going straight was all it took for me to crave the excitement of thieving, so when J.A. managed to get hold of what we called 'Double-Enders' (skeleton keys for Mortice locks), I was once again raring to get back at it. I took these keys from J.A. with the intention of trying them to see how they performed, before attempting to use them on a bigger, riskier job.

So late one evening in December of 1965, under the cover of darkness, I decided to see if they'd open the lock on the door of a high class grocery store and lo and behold they did. Now if I'd been sensible, I'd have relocked the door and gone home, happy in the knowledge that the keys were good for the job and planned something properly. However, my thieving compulsion one again got the better of me and dragged me inside the shop. I surmised...the door was open...the shop was full of stuff...why not...seemed silly not to! I had an old van outside that I'd nicked and rung some days earlier, so transport was no problem. The shop was stuffed with luxury foods, as this was a store that catered for a high class clientele. Also it was just prior to Christmas, so I helped myself to a trolley and pushed it around the store, loading it with salmon, sides of bacon, coffees, beautiful gateaux and puddings, brandies, malt whiskies, wines, top quality cheeses. You name it, I nicked it. The van was well loaded with goodies as I drove to J.A.'s house in Potters Bar to let him know how good the keys where.

I knocked on J.A.'s door armed with these goodies and his wife, who was a lovely lady, opened the door. I screamed "Happy Christmas" and presented her with her luxury hamper! She was thrilled and we went inside, where we all had a good laugh about my shopping trip. J.A. and myself were excited about the potential possibilities with these keys, as we were fairly certain they'd work on the Mortice lock of fairly basic safes.

We only had the use of the keys for a short while before having to return them to a chap who went by the slightly comical nickname of Polish Alf, who they had been hired from, so we devised a little scam which became known as 'The Dinner Time Nip'. This was so called because we used to let ourselves into shops (which in those days, generally closed for an hour) while the staff were out having their lunch, safe in the knowledge that the morning's takings would still be on the premises. These 'Dinner Time Nips' netted us a nice few quid, until Polish Alf took the keys back for his own uses.

By this time Wendy had become increasingly aware of my lifestyle. I generally tried to keep as much of my activities as I could away from her, but she was an intelligent lady and was nobody's fool. Hence, for sometime she had been on at me to curb my criminal activities and to be honest, who could blame her. We were never destitute, as far as money went, at least while I wasn't in prison, but she obviously didn't want to spend her life trying to bring up three children with me in and out constantly. So, in an effort to distance myself from the villainy, a decision was made to move away from the area where I'd lived and been criminally active. In fact, towards the tail end of my sentence in the Scrubs, relocation to a one of the 'new towns' had been suggested to me by the authorities.

Basingstoke in Hampshire was one of these new towns built with the purpose of housing London's overspill and with many large companies relocating there, opportunities of a job and decent housing were excellent. Apparently the schools were excellent too, so Wendy began to make serious enquiries about sorting out a house for us. We made several trips there and were excited about what the future held for us. Even though I had been a criminal all my life from a very young age, I had always worked hard at my regular job. I had never totally relied on my income from villainy. If I said I would take on a building contract, I would always make sure it was completed. Therefore I was keen to secure employment prior to our move, for a fresh start, nice and straight and to this end I was offered a job with a company in my old trade of engineering. A nice family house went with the job as an added bonus, so all looked good.

CHAPTER NINE
BASINGSTOKE

Wendy, myself and the kids moved to Basingstoke early in 1966 and I started work at the engineering company. The kids took to Basingstoke well and loved the open spaces and fields to play in. Even now Basingstoke is relatively small, the countryside being a very short drive away in any direction.

I found the switch back to engineering fairly easy and within an hour of restarting, I'd slipped back into it even though I had been out of the trade for several years, but the set-up at the company was not ideal. I seemed to be the only worker there with any tools and was constantly being asked for a loan of this spanner or that drill, invariably not receiving them back and as I loaned out so many, I couldn't remember who had what. I soon tired of this, aside from the fact that my tools were precious to me, it also made my work difficult as I often needed a tool myself that had gone walkabout. I tried hard to ignore this inconvenience, but I just couldn't get along there, so when the opportunity of a job with a building company arose, I jumped at the chance. There was plenty of building work still going on in Basingstoke as it grew and developed and good tradesmen were very much in demand.

As I mentioned previously, our house went with the engineering job, so in reality I should have surrendered the keys when I resigned, but I decided to front it out and see what happened. As no mention of it was made when I left, I reasoned that it would take them some months to realise the situation before they tried to get us out, giving me time to find alternative accommodation for the family. To my relief, that's exactly what happened. I had found a nice place to rent and was at the negotiating stage when the engineering company realised I was still living in their house. We soon settled into the new place and I was keeping busy with my work as a builder.

I had somehow managed to keep my nose relatively clean since our move to Hampshire, but temptation soon got the better of me. Somehow a trouble free, straight life wasn't for me and yet again, I missed that buzz. I teamed back up with J.A. and another couple of villains and on various trips down to visit me, we began to look for potential targets. The Basingstoke Council Offices seemed to show promise, as we had been handed information which suggested a large vaulted office would contain a substantial amount of cash. A new Police station, (which at that time was still unmanned), was being built opposite the office, so the top floor of this would be a great vantage point for a lookout while we broke in. We suspected there would be a night watchman, so we obtained some old uniform jackets from a surplus store which under the cover of night looked very similar to Police tunics. We figured these would stop him raising the alarm, at least until we got close enough to restrain him. In fact our assumption was wrong and there wasn't a night watchman at all, so we managed to gain entry to the offices without too much effort.

Once inside we began to make our way to the intended target, however en route we passed through the rent office which contained a small safe. My old 'Peterman Head' clicked into gear again and thinking this may also contain cash, I decided to have a pop at it.

I set everything up as usual, unfortunately for some reason when the gelignite went off, the lock jammed. Once that happens, all's lost without a great deal of work, so we abandoned that idea and moved onto the vault room. I set up the gelignite and detonators, just enough 'geli' to blow the lock without too much noise or damage. All went to plan and the lock blew a treat, however, the back plate on the lock had slid over slightly so the tools I had weren't quite sufficient to force the door. I sent J.A. over to the Police station building site opposite to try to get hold of a putlock, (a short section of scaffold tubing with a flat end) which could be used as a large makeshift chisel. He returned with this and with a bit of brute force and ignorance, it managed to do the job, we were in, not that it done us any good. There was absolutely no cash in the vault whatsoever, bad information yet again. All it contained was masses of paperwork, mainly deeds of shops, houses and offices owned by the Council. By now we had been inside for a considerable time, so thought it wise to get out. We didn't want to outstay our welcome, particularly as we had netted absolutely zero from the job.

Anyway shortly afterwards, J.A. came down for a visit with another London villain by the name of 'Mickey', who we had worked with in the past. We all went off to a local pub for a drink and the subject of our bungled Council office job came up in conversation. We had a laugh about it and they went off back to London and I thought no more of it.

A few days later, while out and about in Basingstoke, I was arrested and taken to the Police Station. While I was being held there, they went to my house with a search warrant, Wendy was in and they gave the place a thorough going over. I had several tool grips stored in the garage at my house; one for my decorating work, one for plumbing and a third for electrical tools. The Police had taken these away with them during their search.

I was then taken to identify them in a yard at the Police station and the Detective Sergeant asked me if they were my property, I agreed they were and he proceeded to pull a spent detonator from my electrical bag. This had obviously been found on their search of the Council offices after the robbery and he'd planted it in one of the holdalls. I was livid, snatched it from him and threw it, telling him that there was no way it was mine. This was retrieved by his sidekick and I was charged with the break in and causing an explosion.

This was now serious, causing an explosion can carry a life sentence, so I decided to sound out the D.S. to see if he could be bought. I asked him how much he'd need to forget all about it, but he was having none of it. I feared the worst, but shortly afterwards he approached me with an offer; he said that if I held my hands up to the break-in, no mention would be made of use of explosives. I wasn't sure how I felt about this, and I didn't know whether I trusted him, so sought the advice of my solicitor. He advised me that I had little choice other than trusting him, so with a little trepidation accepted his offer.

I appeared at Winchester Crown Court on 28th December 1966 and was sentenced to five years imprisonment which came to be served at Dartmoor. To this day I'm still not absolutely certain how they put me in the frame for this job, but I have a pretty good idea.

The aforementioned 'Mickey' who came down to Basingstoke with JA, had actually married the also aforementioned and promiscuous Mary (Wendy's neighbour) whose mother, I later found out, was a grass. I'm fairly certain that after my pub conversation with J.A. and Mickey, he'd mentioned it to Mary which then found it's way to her mother. Some years later my suspicions were more or less confirmed when I saw Mary's blabbing mother having a rather serious looking conversation in a Woolworths store, with a C.I.D. officer of my previous acquaintance.

CHAPTER TEN
DARTMOOR

Dartmoor is a large foreboding looking prison near to Princetown, in the county of Devon. Apparently it used to have a carved wooden sign above the door which read "Abandon Hope All Ye Who Enter Here". I'm not sure whether this is a myth or not, if it is, I was to see why it became one!

I arrived here after a short time in Bristol Prison for allocation. Part of the allocation process was going in front of various officials (i.e. the Prison Governor, Psychologist and Psychiatrist) for them to decide which prison to send you to. The inmate who saw the Psychiatrist before me managed to mark my card as he left his office. He reckoned he was either a poof, a pervert or both, as all he wanted to know was the ins and outs of his sex life. What that has to do with which prison you go to, I've no idea, so as far as my fellow inmate's suspicions are concerned, I was inclined to agree with him. I avoided all his dodgy questions and to be honest, it seemed to me it was all a waste of time, as everybody on a long sentence at Bristol prison seemed to get shipped to Dartmoor anyway.

I arrived not really knowing what to expect. The prison has a fearsome reputation. It was originally built in the early 1800's and used to house prisoners from the Napoleonic Wars and then American Seamen from the American War of 1812. At that time it was reputed to have held 6,500 prisoners. Unrest and rioting have been regular occurrences throughout history at Dartmoor, many of them resulting from the quality or lack of food. In fact, one such uprising occurred in 1932, when a horse and cart delivering bread to the prison was attacked as soon as it entered the gate, the prisoners devouring it's contents, such was their hunger.

I knew that some of my muckers, including J.A. were already here and they had discovered I was on my way there too. To make my reception there as pleasant as possible, they had managed to sort me out some decent uniform clothing. It was relatively clean and tidy, compared to the filthy, unpressed rubbish they generally issue you with upon arrival. For this I was extremely grateful, switching from your own neat clothing to the filthy prison uniforms is never nice, to say the least and also, to see some familiar faces also made things a little easier to bear.

Frank Mitchell, who had become known as 'The Mad Axeman' had escaped some months earlier from Dartmoor and the story was still on everybody's lips. He used to work on outside parties and on one of these work outings he was whisked away never to return. The truth of the story is still open to many differing theories which are well documented elsewhere, but the tales concerning this giant of a man and his exploits in Dartmoor soon became well known to me. The immense strength and volatile temper of Mitchell caused him to be given a wide berth by both inmates and screws alike. Apparently if an inmate was caught in possession of anything he shouldn't have, all that was needed was to say,

"it's not mine Guv', I'm looking after it for Frank" and they'd be left alone. On another such instance, when reporting back for return to the prison after an outside work party, Frank was carrying a 21" TV under his arm. When told that he couldn't take it back inside,

Frank replied "We'll see about that".

Later that evening Frank was watching TV in his cell!

Anyway, I attempted to settle in and pass my time as easily as I could. There were some real characters there who I gradually came to know, whose exploits were hilarious and lightened the mood of the place at times. One of these was a gypsy guy known as 'Blackie', as he had jet black curly hair and dark skin. Blackie worked in the kitchens and regularly played practical jokes on anybody and everybody. One of his favourites was to smear blood from the raw liver all over his face and then show himself to the screws who fell for it every time, assuming there had been a stabbing or slashing and flying into a mad panic. Another classic was when he hid himself in one of the enormous steel vats used for cooking vegetables or porridge etc., this happened when he knew the Governor was on one of his regular kitchen visits to check on the food standard. The governor entered the kitchen and proceeded to open up the vats, as he lifted the lid of the first one, Blackie rose up and screamed at the top of his voice, covered in the contents of the container. The poor old Governor nearly had a heart attack. The screws accompanying him could barely contain their laughter.

The two screws who supervised the kitchens used to run a book as an illegal sideline, allowing inmates to have a bet. One day, two hundred quid went missing from their secret stash of betting money and one of these screws, known as Arthur approached me and informed me that he knew all about a brew of hooch (self-made booze) that was fermenting in the corner of the vegetable storeroom. He took great delight in letting me know that as revenge for the missing money, he had urinated in this hooch. As much as I was inclined to let the chaps know, I thought it best to keep quiet, as they may well have wondered how I found out, possibly believing I was a little too close to the screws. Shortly afterwards, I was hearing stories of how wonderful the hooch was, how they had all enjoyed a good drink. If only they knew.

Another inmate there was a strange fella who was known by the nickname 'Hungry Horace'. This poor soul attracted quite a lot of attention at mealtimes. He must have had an eating disorder, as he used to consume vast quantities of whatever pudding was being served that day. They were prepared in trays which measured 24" wide x 18" long and about 6" deep, the pudding was usually a stodgy duff or spotted dick and Hungry Horace would have no trouble whatsoever in consuming a tray of this muck. Inmates sat around him, transfixed and amazed as he shovelled this dense mass of pudding down, mouthful by mouthful. He looked eight months pregnant by the time he'd finished, then he'd proceed to the toilet and spew the lot up. Nowadays I think this would be recognised as bulimia, but back then we just thought he was a greedy git!

My first job at Dartmoor was at a quarry. We'd be taken out under escort to a quarry to break what I thought was rocks. Having being issued with a leather apron, goggles and an enormous sledgehammer, I set to work attempting to smash up these rocks. After about half an hour, I'd made very little impression on any of these. A lovely old civilian who was in charge of this work came over when he saw me struggling and explained that these 'rocks' were in fact lumps of granite. Granite has a grain running through it and they need hitting along the grain, they then split along this grain. He demonstrated and I soon got the knack, my job was somewhat easier from then, but still very physical work.

However, Tommy Black, an old safe blower who had become a good pal of mine, (due to us having so much in common!), operated the crusher which the pieces of granite were fed into and he recommended me to take over his duties, as he was due for release. Luckily, they took me on. This was far less strenuous, thanks Tommy.

During our working day at the quarry, a Land Rover would arrive from the prison with our lunches, usually sandwiches of some sort. I had a fella in the kitchen straightened out and he used to put a large container of milk and some of yesterdays bread rolls onboard for me. During the day, afternoon usually, I'd toast up these rolls and brew some tea for the selected few, in the hut which housed the crusher. It was a welcome break for the lads, however there was an unpopular welshman, nicknamed 'Taffy' (what else!) who we deliberately left out of these sessions. He knew the score, but he was either thick or thick-skinned, I'm not sure which, but he would always open the door, stick his head in and in his broad welsh accent, say "Can I smell toast Boyos?" Day after day of being told to "fuck off Taff" didn't seem to deter him either. He'd still be back the next afternoon again and again. Until one day we surprised him and invited him in. Little did he know we really did have a surprise in store for him. This hut was regularly invested with mice, which we attempted to thump with our boots, occasionally succeeding. This particular day was one of those occasions, fortunately for us and UNFORTUNATELY for poor old Taff. After making himself comfortable next to the stove, we presented him with a toasted roll filled with a nice, freshly killed mouse inside.

"There's loveleee" exclaimed Taff as he went to bite into his roll. Just as he sunk his teeth into it, a great long tail slipped out the side. Taff hadn't noticed, but everybody else had. The laughter erupted, Taff finally saw the tail, the roll flew up into the air and Taff flew out the door screaming. I'm not sure whether he'd actually got a mouthful of mouse, but strangely enough, he didn't bother us again!

As mentioned previously, Tommy Black became a very good friend and I was sorry to see him go, but obviously also pleased for him that he was on his way out. Before he was released we brewed up some top quality hooch in the stables. Ponies were kept at Dartmoor then, as the screws rode them on patrol around the prison. We used to groom the ponies and therefore had regular access to the stables. We had managed to get hold of quality ingredients from 'our man' in the kitchen and the warm atmosphere of the stable was perfect for brewing. I've no idea what the actual strength of this stuff was, but believe me it was STRONG. I gave a bottle of it to a pal of mine who had cause to visit the stable while I was there one day, he was pissed for three days solid, didn't know where he was!

While I was on this stable job, I'd managed to work out some lovely little perks for myself. I've always taken great pride in my fitness and part of my duties was to accompany the tractor driver in maintaining the many fields surrounding the prison. There were so many of these fields, gated individually, that I'd run in front of the tractor to open the gates. This kept me in tip-top nick. While on these outings, I'd noticed lovely large trout in the many streams in the area. As we reached one of these streams one day, I called out to Ernie the tractor driver to stop for a while. I went over to the edge of the stream and the trout were so plentiful, I could literally pull them out. This became a regular thing, we'd take some back and Tommy would cook them up. As the food at Dartmoor wasn't that good, (as at most prison's, to my extensive experience!) these fish dinners were most welcome.

Another time, whilst working on a different outside working party, we took great advantage of a lovely old screw's nice, but highly gullible nature. He'd just started on this party and he was a good natured old soul, but needs must as they say. At break time, I asked him for permission to go to the stream to fetch a bucketful of beautiful, clear water to brew our tea with. This was granted and off I went, returning shortly afterwards with my bucket of water and another bucket full of lovely trout. The old screw was astounded,

"How d'you get them Mick?"

"Just snatched them straight from the stream Guv'", I replied, "D'you fancy one? They're lovely!"

Immediately he came back with, "Not 'arf".

Now he was mine, I had him! I gutted and cleaned the trout, then grilled them in a bit of butter on the stove in our rest hut. The screw couldn't get it down his neck quick enough. As he was licking his lips afterwards, I told him we did this on a daily basis and that he could have trout every day for his lunch if he liked. He was well pleased at this prospect, that's when I hit him with the punchline;

"The last screw on this working party used to bring out some eggs and bacon for our breakfast, in return for trout for his lunch Guv'", I lied.

I definitely had him now!

"No problem Mick, I'll sort that".

We ate like kings on that party for several weeks, sadly I was shifted to another job and my 'a la carte' dining came to an end.

Generally the screws at Dartmoor were fairly reasonable blokes, but there's always an exception to the rule isn't there? A prime example of this, was when I decided I'd like a radio in my cell. I asked my landing's screw for permission, which really should have been granted without any fuss. Now this particular screw was one horrible, miserable little jobsworth and he insisted that I needed a licence before he'd grant permission. I pointed out that any individual house or dwelling only needed ONE licence to cover all TVs and radios in that particular place, but he wasn't having it. I asked him to check, which he obviously didn't because if he had, he'd have discovered that I was right. So he continued to refuse permission. This disagreement continued until I finally caved in and purchased a radio licence with my own little bit of savings from my work in the nick. Finally, I got my radio and enjoyed the diversion that listening to music and plays gave me. Some weeks later, I was delighted when reading the area's local paper, to see an article relating to a resident of nearby Princetown, who had been nicked for not having a TV licence. Guess who it was? That's right...the miserable git who wouldn't allow me a radio until I'd bought a licence! As much as this injustice riled me, it pleased me even more. I let all the boys on the landing know and didn't we give him some stick...for weeks on end. Lovely...karma I think they call it.

Prison's are miserable places and anything that can lighten that situation is always very welcome, anything at all that takes your mind off your surroundings for a while. Visits from friends and family are obviously really looked forward to. Unfortunately, with Dartmoor being so far to travel for Wendy and the kids, it wasn't very practical, therefore my visits were few and far in between. However, on the occasions they did occur I tried to make the best of them, but it was fairly clear how Wendy felt about me getting myself in this situation again. It was entirely of my own making, with no-one else to blame. How poor Wendy put up with it all, I'll never know.

Before old Tommy Black was released, a funny thing happened when he had a visit from a nephew of his. Tommy was working on the prison dustcart at the time, which used to leave the prison grounds to clear the rubbish bins from outside the screws' houses, which were in the nearby village. On the visit, he asked this nephew to come down on a particular day and leave a parcel hidden behind a rock near the cricket ground. The parcel was to contain tobacco, toiletries etc. Obviously, his job would allow him to retrieve this on his rounds. Unfortunately, his dear nephew was a little naive about the workings of the prison mail system, as in his next letter he enclosed a photograph of the exact hiding place of said parcel. Tommy was called up to the Governor's office and informed about this, but strangely enough he was given all his goodies. I've no idea why, some technicality or the other I assume.

Another little perk of Tommy's dustcart job came to light soon after this incident. Pornography is not allowed in prison and if found, it's confiscated. Now one day. while Tommy's on his rounds he tipped out a dustbin into the cart and there amongst the rubbish are several porno magazines. It transpired that the screws were taking home the confiscated magazines for their own enjoyment and when they were finished with them, threw them out. So dear old Tommy, being ever so green and eco-friendly, recycled them back to whence they came, straight into the prison again!

Around this time, other working parties were being taken out to maintain and decorate prison officer's houses. One of the inmates in this party, who had become a good friend of mine, was a chap by the name of Peter Gulston, better known as Peter Scott, his nickname being 'King of the Cat Burglars', as he'd became infamous for stealing celebrities jewellery (Sophia Loren, Zsa Zsa Gabor and Vivien Leigh amongst them). In fact a film based on his exploits was released while he was in Dartmoor, 'He Who Rides A Tiger'. Peter was a real character, originally from a well-to-do family in Belfast. He claimed that "he had been sent by God to take back some of the wealth that the outrageously rich have taken from the rest of us". How good a mission statement is that? During the compiling of this book I was saddened to hear of his death, which occurred in March 2013 at the age of 82. Sleep tight Peter.

Whilst in one of the houses on one of these working parties, another inmate struck up a conversation with a pretty wife of a prison officer. She brought the conversation round to the subject of pornography in the prison and stated that she was very curious about it as she'd never seen any. She asked if he could bring some for her to see. He duly obliged and whether it was the porn that made her fruity or whether she just took a fancy to him I don't know, but they were soon having sex. However, they were disturbed by a T.A. (a civilian Trades Assistant), who supervised the inmates work and to cover her actions, she claimed he was raping her. He had his sentence increased by three years.

Dartmoor is in a remote part of Dartmoor National Park and was liable to be hit by some extremely severe weather. One winter towards the end of my sentence, the prison was surrounded by 18 foot snow drifts. The mail and meat supplies had to be flown in by helicopter, but the potatoes, bread and other vegetables etc. could not be transported by this method due to the vast weight of the quantities required. They had managed to get them by road, as far as the Dartmoor Inn, a large pub and hotel some miles away. Being an outside party worker, I was sent with five other inmates, on a large crawler tractor to attempt to get some supplies back to the 'nick'. When we eventually arrived at the Inn, a Landrover was parked up stranded, with four screws inside shivering. We hitched this vehicle up and towed them back to the prison, then set off again for the inn and the food supplies. By the time we reached the pub, we were all almost frozen stiff, as we were not kitted out with any sort of proper winter clothing.

Before our return journey, the staff at the inn took us into the boiler room to thaw out. A table was laid out there and we were each given a pint of Barley Wine and a lovely plate of steak and chips. This was a real treat and set us up for the arduous journey back to the prison, towing a large trailer loaded with food. We eventually arrived back at the prison, thinking we were going to be congratulated as heroes. However, the following day we were the laughing stock of the nick. It transpired that the stranded Landrover we had towed back, not only contained the four screws BUT also the entire, three hundred strong prison staff's wage packets! It became known as the Mafia Outing!

Another funny incident occurred, when we were on a working party just outside the prison, building an additional car park for visitors and staff. We were just finishing up for the day and making our way back, when a coach party came along. This happened regularly, as part of their tour of Dartmoor National Park, they were shown the prison. These coach parties were known to us as the 'Rubberneckers'. We were carrying large chains that were used to lock up our heavy tools with, now I thought it'd be a great idea to give the rubberneckers a bit of a show. So I got all the lads to hang these chains around their necks and chant away as we walked back to the main gate.

"OOH-AAH, OOH-AHH" we went as we marched in unison. The rubberneckers loved it, their camera shutters were going ten to the dozen. Even the screws saw the funny side of it.

Another similar incident involving the rubberneckers occurred one day, as the coach came past a pony party from the prison was returning and awaiting the gates being opened for them. An inmate on the party, walking alongside one of the ponies was patting this pony's stomach, well this animal was obviously finding this patting rather erotic, as he now had the biggest hard-on of his life. The coach drove past, stopped briefly, reversed for a better look and once again the camera shutters were working overtime.

Little jokes and these occasional incidents lifted our spirits, anything that was a break from the monotony of the same old daily routine really. Anyway, the exceptionally cold winter passed and as I was nearing the end of my time, I was to be sent to the working out hostel in Pentonville Prison.

This was a wing, totally separate from the main prison where you served the last few months of your sentence, however you were allowed out to work. The job was found for you and as long as you kept your nose clean for your time there, all would be well for your eventual release. This was intended to reintegrate inmates back into society gradually, rather than the initial shock of being slung back out and left to your own devices after a long spell inside. It's thought that convicts were less likely to immediately re-offend this way.

For the transfer to Pentonville from Dartmoor, there was myself, a old 'blagger' (armed robber) who was a lovely bloke, called Bonzo and a 'courtesy' prison officer, who was assigned to accompany us on the train journey and then on the final leg to the hostel. We were allowed the dignity of all three of us being dressed in civilian clothes rather than uniforms, if you could call the cheap old tat they'd issued me and Bonzo with dignified. God knows what material the suits were made from, but once you'd sat down for no more than two minutes, they looked like screwed up dish cloths. We had also been given the option of a hat and as it was raining, we both chose the rather nasty looking flat caps. As bad as they were, we reckoned they looked better than the ridiculous limp brimmed trilbies on offer. Not that it made any difference really, we looked ridiculous and we knew it. I reckon the general public thought we'd just got out from a time warp in the 1940's!

After being dropped at Tavistock station by mini-bus and while waiting for the train, Bonzo asked me to divert the attention of the screw for a minute or two, to enable him to ring his wife. This I managed by telling him I needed to use the toilet and trusting Bonzo more than me I guess, he accompanied me to the gents while old Bonz' rang his missus, told her which train we were catching and asked her to meet us at the station. I seem to recall it was Paddington.

Old Bonzo had me in stitches on the journey. After about an hour, he stood up for a stretch, everybody in the busy carriage watched as he stretched his arms out to his sides as he made that straining noise that we all make. Then as calm and as natural as you like, he opened the window, took off his flat cap and flung it straight out of the window like a frisbee! He then sat back down with a complete deadpan expression on his face as though this was the most natural thing in the world. Didn't everybody throw flat caps out of train windows? He got some strange looks from our fellow passengers, I can tell you. Even my howling with laughter had no effect on him, he didn't crack a smile. I often wonder what happened to old Bonzo.

As we left the train, we asked if we could get a cup of tea, as we'd had absolutely nothing on the long journey. He wasn't keen initially, but relented and off we went to the cafeteria. The screw took a seat at a table and we joined the queue, at which point my pal's wife joined us and told us to load up on whatever we wanted. This we did, grateful for her offer and had a large main course and pudding each. We then went to join our courtesy screw at his table. He looked gutted.

"How d'you manage to get all that?" he asked.

"We were lucky enough to bash into someone we knew", came the reply.

He sat and watched and we tucked in. I was sure I saw him salivating. It was only sometime later, while in the hostel, we found out he had actually been given seven pounds each to feed and water us on the train. The greedy sod had used it to beer it up at our expense in the bar of the buffet carriage. Typical, but we got a nice meal anyway, thanks to 'Mrs. Bonzo'.

Afterwards, we continued our journey onto Pentonville and were admitted to the hostel. Due to my previous work experience, I was allocated to a job with a large decorating contractors. Initially, I was sent on a large painting contract at a cigarette manufacturers over in south London, which was ironic really as I had spent a lot of time thieving ciggies and tobacco. I managed to stay out of trouble, worked well and was promoted to foreman.

I was then transferred and worked night shifts at the Strand Palace and Regent's Palace hotels, supervising the redecoration teams at both venues. I was thankful for the opportunity and took my work seriously. I have always been a conscientious worker, striving for the best possible result of my efforts.

While stripping hessian wallpaper at the Strand Palace one night, the restaurant manager approached me and told me how he'd love the same paper in his house. Now, this hessian wall covering, if taken off carefully, can actually be reused. I told him this and rolled the stripped paper up for him to take home. In return, he allowed me and the other lads to have a night feast of all the roast joints of meat and potatoes left over at the end of service in the carvery restaurant. So each night, when I knocked the lads off at 4.30am, we'd have a real slap-up meal before shooting off. Nice! After the dreadful Dartmoor food and the still pretty ropey fare at Pentonville, this was a real treat.

As we finished our meal one night, a young Scottish painter who the company had recently allocated to my supervision, picked up his jacket to leave and about 100 knives and forks fell out of his pockets onto the floor. He hung his head in shame as I told him to put them back. I had to stifle a smile though, the workers under me had no idea of my status as an ex-convict. As far as they were concerned, I was just their foreman.

I saw some goings on in those hotels, particularly as I was there throughout the night. I recall I was painting some skirting boards in the reception of the Strand Palace one night, when I heard two pairs of feet in high heels clip clopping along at what sounded like high speed. I looked up just in time, to catch sight of two attractive young ladies disappearing out of the front door. I thought no more of it, until several minutes later a portly middle-aged chap dressed in nothing more than his underpants came storming into reception, claiming he'd been robbed. It didn't take Einstein to figure out who his 'guests' were and why they also happened to take his trousers, along with a bulging wallet, no doubt!

CHAPTER ELEVEN
OUT AGAIN.....BRIEFLY!

When my designated time at the hostel was up I moved back to Basingstoke with Wendy and the kids. This was late in 1969 and I'd served just over 3 years of my five year sentence. I continued to work at the hotels, for the same decorating contractors for a short time, but travelling back and forth each night was a chore and before long I got myself a job in the same trade, but locally, for a Basingstoke based company.

Any prison sentence takes it's toll on a marriage and mine was no exception. It took time to get things back to normal, but I was determined to make my marriage work and go straight. I realise now how farcical this sounds, considering how many times I've stated the same sound bite previously in this book. Especially as very shortly after my release I was back inside for another five year sentence, which I'll get to later in this chapter, but at the time I thought I was serious about going straight and settling down. If only I had known how different my life could have been. Looking back now, I realise there was a certain inevitability about my destiny and future. I've tried convincing myself I was doing all the villainy to secure financial security for my family by getting rich quick, however, realistically I think it was the lifestyle and buzz that crime gave me was more motivational than any monetary reward. I apologise for repeating myself, but how poor Wendy put up with it all I'll never know. That lady was, and still is a saint as far as I'm concerned!

I was struggling somewhat financially during this short period of freedom after Dartmoor and decided to call in a debt from J.A. This was from a job we had pulled off sometime earlier, from which I was still owed a share. I drove over to his house at Potters Bar with a view to recover this money. There was no bad feeling between us over this, it was purely financial. However, on arrival at his place he informed me that he was in no position to be able to pay me my dues. J.A. had always been a serious boozer, consuming a bottle and a half of Scotch on an almost daily basis, so money didn't last too long in his wallet.

However, he had recently been casing a Post Office, close by in Potter's Bar and put the job to me as an easy touch. He reckoned we could break in using our trademark method of through the ceiling, 'geli' the safe, hoping to get to the cash and postal orders. JA already had the rubber stamps to be able to authorise these P.O.'s from a previous job, so we were hoping for a good haul.

Bang went my resolution to keep on the straight and narrow, I took very little persuasion and told him I was up for it. We set about planning it and took a trip to have a look around. You'll probably be thinking "What the hell was he thinking, literally just out of prison and re-offending almost immediately?" at this moment and my answer would be "I've no idea!" I really have absolutely no answer or possible explanation for my behaviour. Sure, I was desperate for money at that time, but so are so many other people at times in their life, without resorting to crime. I was probably just a compulsive thief.

This little sub Post Office had a flat roof above it with a standard felt covering, which wouldn't be difficult to get through. The safe was in view from the counter and was situated at the back of the shop.

We set about the job one night with the plan of breaking through the felt roof and cutting through the ceiling joists to allow just enough room to squeeze through into the post office. This progressed to plan and we thought we were onto a winner. However, unbeknown to us, alarm wires had been run along the ceiling which we had broken. This had triggered an alarm which was silent in the post office, however it was probably ringing off the wall in the local nick. Before we managed to get our hands an anything of any value, we were nicked...again! This was 9th January 1970, I seem to recall that it was literally only a matter of weeks after my release from the hostel in Pentonville. I was sentenced to five years at Hertfordshire Quarter Sessions on the 9th March.

CHAPTER TWELVE
ALBANY

After a short period in Brixton for allocation, I was taken over to the Isle of Wight in April 1970 to serve my sentence in Albany Prison. It had been built only a few years earlier, however being a modern building didn't make the conditions much better to be honest. The tension there was almost tangible, there was absolutely no relationship between inmates and staff. Prisons, by their very nature, are obviously not the happiest of places and Albany, at that time was certainly top of the 'unhappy league'.

Amongst the inmates there at the time was Charlie Kray who had been implicated alongside his brothers in the murder of Jack 'The Hat' McVitie. I got on well with him, he was a lovely guy and to be honest I felt sorry for him. He constantly spoke of how the only real thing he was guilty of was being 'a brother to the twins'.

Shortly after arriving, I was put to work in the mail bag workshop where I was taught to operate a sewing machine. I found the work boring and monotonous and as far I could see, I wasn't alone in feeling this way, which didn't help the already explosive atmosphere. Fights would start at the slightest little thing and I could almost see the tension building up and up. I felt it wouldn't be too long before some serious trouble occurred and I was right, it kicked off into an almighty riot. This started off when an inmate had his cell searched by staff. He was due to be released in a matter of days and had spent some considerable time making a beautiful lined wooden jewellery box as a present for his wife. These 'screws' wrecked this box in sheer spite and obviously the inmate remonstrated with them. He was marched to the punishment block where he was given a severe beating.

News spreads quickly in prison and before long all hell had broken loose. For some days, the whole prison was in uproar. As always with these things, it eventually settled down, however the situation and conditions were still pretty bad. Queues of inmates were outside the Governor's office on a daily basis with various complaints and grievances.

The nature of these complaints were usually on the same points:-
Visits; Prison staff being rude and abusive to inmates families on visits.
Clothing; Inmates' personal clothing (i.e. trainers and t-shirts) had been confiscated and the clothing we were forced to wear was dreadful.
Food; We hardly expected Michelin star restaurant food, but at least edible would be nice.
Staff; The general lack of any semblance of a relationship between staff and inmates.

This continued for a while until the Chief Warder eventually approached the Governor with a plan of action. He could see that the whole system in Albany was just not working and after much thought and many meetings (some with staff only, others included inmates), they decided that an inmate from each of the six wings would be designated as a representative to voice any problems or views that were brought to his notice. I was asked to step forward for my particular wing, to which I agreed. I was issued with a large book and inmates would approach me with their complaints which I duly noted. A weekly meeting would then be held, attended by all six wing representatives, the Governor and the Chief Warder and we would bring up and attempt to iron out all complaints etc. On the whole, I felt that this was working to a certain extent. At least it was an improvement on the previous situation. However, this situation certainly didn't suit everyone, as I found out to my cost. The food had improved somewhat, but still wasn't great and some inmates had decided to make an impromptu demonstration in the dining halls.

This had been instigated in my wing by an inmate called 'Big' Chris. Chris had put a couple of big lads on the door of the dining hall to stop and 'persuade' the inmates to join the protest by not eating the food. I was informed of this and went down to see what was happening. As I approached the door, the lad minding it, who I knew, informed me that the food was rubbish and that no-one was going to eat. I told him that I would at least need to taste it, if anything constructive was going to come of this protest. I went through and tried the food. I felt there had been some improvement, but it was still of a pretty poor standard, which I noted in the book to be brought up at the next meeting. I later found out that I was the only inmate to eat anything at that mealtime. However, I had only eaten in an effort to gather information to be able to report my findings.

Later that night on association, an inmate came up to my cell and informed me that a guy called Fred wanted to see me. I knew Fred and assumed he wanted to see me with regard to my representative duties, so I made my way to his cell. As I entered, I saw that Chris was there with several other guys. I was told in no uncertain terms that they thought I had screwed up their protest by tasting the food and while I was held still, Chris beat me to a pulp. My prison shirt was sodden with blood. My face was battered so badly it swelled up like a balloon. After the beating I managed to stagger along the landing to my cell where I made a half-hearted attempt to clean myself up. A screw came along at one point and on seeing the state of my face, asked me what had happened. I told him I'd fallen down the stairs, he obviously didn't believe it but knew I'd say no more. I was taken out to a hospital where I spent some time recuperating from this serious beating.

On my return into Albany, the atmosphere was still dreadful. There were some decent Prison Officers there, but on the whole they were absolute bastards, whose main object in life was to make life as difficult and miserable as possible for the inmates. I know some readers will be thinking that prison is there as a deterrent and that it shouldn't be a pleasant experience. I agree, but there is a big difference between being punished and being treated like an animal.

A prime example of this occurred one day unfortunately, when something I'd eaten had upset my stomach, (there's that dodgy food again!) which was causing me to experience severe stomach cramps. I was desperate to use the toilet, however it was out of the designated time for this. I explained my plight to the landing screw, a Mr. Jones who told me to lock myself in my cell and that as soon as everybody was put to work, I'd be allowed to use the toilet. Work was due to start shortly, so I accepted this and put myself into my cell and pulled the door closed, which locks automatically, making the door inoperable from the inside. I waited and waited, but nobody came to allow me out. I banged on the door, but was totally ignored. The cramps in my stomach were making me double up in pain and how I managed to stop myself soiling myself I'll never know. It was several hours that I was left in this state, until I was eventually let out to relieve myself. I was livid and so determined that I was not going to let this pass, surely treating a person in this manner was inhuman.

My opportunity arose a day or so later, when the Governor was on one of his kitchen inspections and I was there in my role as wing representative. The Governor (Mr. Footer) was a fairly decent and understanding man, who I had always found to be willing to listen to any grievances I brought to his attention. I explained the situation regarding my stomach problem and he immediately suspended Mr. Jones who had left me in my cell suffering. He carried this out, totally on my word, which tells me that he was well aware of the dreadful treatment some his staff were imposing on inmates.

Another incident springs to mind concerning the complete anarchy that was prevalent in Albany at that time. A high profile inmate named Freddie was there at that time and he'd had a few run-ins with the screws. He filled a very large flask with his own urine and excrement and carried it to the office where around eight screws were sitting having tea, he then proceeded to shower these officers with the contents of the flask. I realise this may sound disgusting behaviour but I think this goes some way to showing how much real hate existed between staff and inmates at that time.

It really was no wonder that serious violence was happening with such frequency. The routine seemed to be a constant battle of wits between screws and inmates, which always seemed to spill over into confrontation.

This continued more or less for my whole sentence, however I managed to avoid as much of it as possible personally. Prison time is unpleasant and my reasoning was 'why make it any more difficult?'

I served around 3 years and 3months in Albany and was released in June of 1973.

Once again, I was sent to the hostel at Pentonville and spent my days out working as a painter/decorator and reporting back to the hostel after work. A friend of mine called Dick Pooley who was also at the hostel at the same time, was actually allocated to work decorating a bank vault, which we both found hilarious as he was a safe blower!

CHAPTER THIRTEEN
BACK HOME.........AGAIN

It was a massive relief to be out and back home with Wendy and the kids in Basingstoke. My daughters Jane and Lucy were now 10 and 8 years old respectively and my son David was 7. Yet again it was difficult for all of them for a while, particularly the younger two, as they were so young when I went into Albany. Initially, we had the same scenario as my previous homecomings, in that the kids were treating me like a complete stranger, but they were great kids and Wendy had been marvellous with them, considering the somewhat difficult circumstances. My relationship with my wife had suffered again during this sentence, as visits had been fairly infrequent. No fault of hers, I might add, Basingstoke to Albany is a difficult undertaking logistically for visits, particularly with three young children to account for. Once again, I did my best to make up for lost time and after a while things began to return to some sort of semblance of normal family life.

I had secured a job with a local builders and decorating company in Basingstoke, and was enjoying the work, as I always had. They were a busy company with plenty of regular contracts and I was managing to keep myself on a fairly straight course. Occasionally a minor little tickle or fiddle with JA would come up, that I would find hard to resist, but on the whole, kept myself busy with legitimate work.

All was going well, for the first time since the kids were born, we were as normal a family as we'd ever been. My relationship with Wendy was good again and she was delighted I was managing to keep my nose clean, relatively! To be honest, I feel that I could have trodden a 'more or less' straight goers life from then on, had it not been for the freak accident had happened, that was to change the course of my life for ever.

I was working on a conversion job, changing an office into a flats and as part of that job, we were ripping out an old fireplace. I had two young lads working under my supervision and when the fireplace was freed up from the wall, I instructed the lads to take it down outside and to cover it over with a tarpaulin, should it be required elsewhere or to be sold on. I left the lads to it and busied myself elsewhere. About 20 minutes later, there was no sign of them, so I went to see where they had got to.

They must have been struggling as they'd barely moved it more than a yard or two and were still having a stupid debate as to how best to go about shifting it. Rather than watch this debacle, I reckoned it would be quicker to do it myself, so put them onto something else and started the journey downstairs with the fireplace. All went to plan, until I had to twist myself around to negotiate a section of stairway and then suddenly....pop! Something went very wrong with my back, I screamed out in pain and sunk to the floor. I had a real problem attempting to get back onto my feet and had to be assisted.

I tried my best to sort myself out with a stretch or two, but it soon became very clear that there was no way I could continue work in this state, so managed to get myself off home (with considerable difficulty) and put myself to bed.

Wendy made me as comfortable as possible, but I was in a great deal of pain. I was praying that it would right itself by the morning, however, if anything it was worse. I had more or less totally seized up and the slightest movement was excruciating. I got myself to my Doctor's somehow and he examined me and diagnosed a slipped disc.

He prescribed a strong Distalgesic based pain killer, which took the edge off the pain but obviously didn't cure the back problem, so any early return to manual labour was out of the question. In fact my GP informed me I took the chance in ending up in a wheelchair if I continued with heavy labour while on these drugs.

I felt totally helpless and spent my days indoors, driving Wendy mad. I had always been an active person and found the inactivity hard to endure, as a result my head was all over the place. I explained this to my GP, on one of my regular check ups and he added Valium to my prescription. The Valium combined with the Distalgesic was a fairly heavy cocktail and I was in a state of semi-consciousness for a while. Once my body adapted slightly, I was able to stay awake, but felt stoned most of the time.

I had a bit of money behind me, but realised that I was likely to be out of the building game for sometime, so began to look for opportunities before I was totally destitute. I knew some guys in the motor trade and managed to fix up a meeting with a Sales Manager from a local main dealer. We came to a deal whereby I would take the older trade-in vehicles that they took in part-exchange off his hands to sell on (hopefully for a profit). Being a main dealer, their business was in new vehicles, so they were glad to offload them as soon as possible.

In an effort to maximise my profits from this enterprise, I perfected the art of rewinding the car's mileometers back by as many thousands as I deemed necessary and possible.

This car dealing continued for sometime and for a while, gave me a reasonable living. After some time though, things began to slow down and I was scratching around again looking for opportunities, sure enough...I was soon back at it and managed to 'get hold' of some uncut diamonds that I was in the process of attempting to sell when I found myself arrested again.

While on bail for this offence, I had to report to a local Police station twice a day to sign on, as a condition of my bail. One day as I entered the Police station, behind the counter, I saw a young lady who I had previously employed on a part time basis to do some typing and clerical work for me, while I was motor trading. She was called Sharon and on spotting me, she called out and asked me if I could help her out. She had been arrested for non-payment of fines and was likely to be jailed unless these fines were paid there and then. She told me that she had the money indoors and if I paid them for her, she would reimburse me. I left the Police Station to withdraw some cash and returned, paid her outstanding fines and she was released.

As we walked away, she admitted to me that she had lied, in fact she did not have access to the money, but would bring me in on her 'kiting', work (the passing of forged or stolen cheques). That began another chapter of my life, initially she was getting hold of cheque books and we worked together as a 'couple', an older man and his 'young girlfriend'. As this progressed, I managed to get hold of more cheque books myself, on a regular basis and we became quite adept at purchasing goods from shops in various areas.

From this, we also began 'The Tweedle', a scam which consisted of entering a jeweller's shop with an assortment of costume jewellery rings of many different shapes and sizes tucked safely away in my pocket. While browsing the trays inside the store, we'd put on an act with me being the sugar daddy and Sharon being my 'bit on the side'. Sharon was an extremely good actress and played the part of the giggly young blonde, excited to be treated to a diamond ring by her older boyfriend. We'd then select a tray of rings containing some that resembled our collection of fakes and ask to see them. The shop assistant would present us with the rings and Sharon would proceed to try a selection on. With a nifty sleight of hand, several genuine rings would be switched for our fakes, the tray then returned to the assistant, Sharon telling her that none had particularly caught her eye and we'd leave with the good stuff tucked safely away in Sharon's bag or my pocket.

Our spoils from these outings had to be sold off as quickly as possible to get the cash, however they also had to be sold to someone reliable. It would have been foolish to sell them off to just anyone, as the chances of it coming back to bite us would have been far greater. A fence I had used previously was always willing to take more or less anything I could put his way, however a side effect of being so reliable, was that the percentage of the retail value that he offered was relatively small. We were earning a decent income, but by the time we shared the cash out and paid travelling expenses, it wasn't a fortune.

What with worrying about this and the way the drugs were making me feel, I just felt as though I really needed to get away for a holiday. I approached Wendy to see how she felt about just the two of us taking some time away, however she wasn't keen on leaving the kids with somebody else. As much as I tried to persuade her, she was having none of it. I explained how desperate I was feeling, so she told me to go on my own. Unbeknown to Wendy, I asked Sharon if she'd like to come, she also declined. So I reasoned, "sod it! I'll go on my own."

CHAPTER FOURTEEN
AMSTERDAM

I started visiting some local travel agents, looking for somewhere suitable for my solitary holiday. I didn't fancy travelling too far, but decided that lounging around on a beach wasn't for me. I needed something and somewhere that would my keep my mind occupied. The drugs were making my mind race, I felt as though my thoughts were at 100mph, sitting idly would be the last thing I needed. Even though I knew very little about it, only what I had seen in books, Amsterdam seemed a great option, numerous things to see and do, the canals, museums and galleries, plenty to keep me occupied.

I booked just my flight, reckoning I would find a hotel once I arrived in Amsterdam, just play it by ear and see what happens was my plan. So off I went, I flew to Schiphol Airport and took a taxi into the centre of Amsterdam and had a wander around looking for somewhere to stay. I didn't have a vast amount of money, in fact I had very little, once again I think the drugs were seriously clouding my judgement. In reality, I had absolutely no chance of having any sort of proper holiday on the cash in my pocket. I did have some more cash in my very first, recently opened bank account, but no idea that I may have been able to withdraw some abroad.

Unaware, (or more likely, ignorant) of my somewhat precarious financial situation, I booked myself into a rather grand looking hotel. Looking back now, I have no idea where it was, other than it seemed to be a very busy district of the city. Showing how naive I was at the time, they quoted me a figure of money per night's stay, I didn't have the foggiest idea how this equated to pounds sterling. Perhaps I should have been alerted by the rather splendid, expensively furnished and decorated rooms that it wasn't going to be cheap. Call it naivety, stupidity or maybe the concoction of chemicals clouding my brain, but within a short period of time, I was going to realise that I would be out of money in no time at all.

I was shown up to my room by a very smartly dressed bell-boy, gave him a tip, (probably far too much, I've no idea!) unpacked my things, showered and changed and decided to have a stroll and get myself a meal.

I spent a nice evening exploring the area and found a lovely restaurant, where I had a slap-up meal and a nice bottle of wine. I paid my bill and I think that was when I first realised how quickly my money would disappear. The following day I spent sight seeing and yet another large hole was dug into my wallet. After paying for my meal that evening, the full reality of my situation was becoming evidently clear. I would have to do something to get some money and the only way I knew how was thieving.

I began to look for an likely opportunity. Not too far from my hotel was a rather plush looking apartment block and after having a good look around, I felt that gaining entry wouldn't cause me too much of a problem, such was my expertise in burglary. There didn't seem to be a concierge or porter in the lobby area to disturb me, so next morning I set about it.

Fortunately, the main door to the block was in a fairly quiet side street and around 11 a.m., reckoning that most of the residents would be out at work, I was able to 'lloid the door (use a thin piece of plastic, similar to a credit card) and gain entry. I crept upstairs, noticing that the doors to the apartments had a glass panel set into them. Some had a light on in the hallway beyond the door, so I dismissed these. I decided to try a door where I could see no light, I knocked and then shot up a flight of stairs out of the way and waited a while. There was no answer, perfect. The door to the apartment opened as easily as the main door with my 'lloid' and I was in. I wanted to spend as little time as possible in there, so took a couple of watches, some rings and a necklace, (items that would fit into my pocket) and left.

Now I had to try to turn them into hard cash. I made my way around local bars and approached guys I thought least likely to worry about the origins of the items, however, either they were all honest men or didn't like the look of me, but I soon realised I was onto a loser. Not too many spoke English either, which didn't help matters. It was now late afternoon and I'd raised next to nothing.

I decided I had no other option but to go home. Realising I didn't have enough money to pay my hotel bill, I had to make sure I left without them realising I would not be returning later that day. I returned to my room and began to pack, however I discarded my small suitcase that I'd come with and used a couple of store carrier bags, so that I looked as though I was just carrying some shopping as I passed through reception.

I managed this without arousing suspicion, probably helped by the amount of guests at the desk as I walked through. A couple were paying off a taxi as I left the hotel, so I hailed him before he shot off and asked for Schiphol airport. He set off and I had to hatch a plan to get out of paying him, as I didn't even have enough for the cab fare. I kept a look out for any sign as to our location with respect to the airport, after a while I saw a road sign stating '5km to Airport'. Thinking quickly I opened the back window of the cab, leant out and made noises as though I was being sick. Hearing this, the cab driver pulled over and got out to see if I was okay. He was wearing very thick lensed glasses, which I snatched from his face and threw down a grass verge. He obviously couldn't see a thing without them, which was evident as he squealed and headed down the verge to retrieve them, stumbling along with his arms in front of him. I quickly jumped from the back seat, hopped into the driver's seat and set off for the airport, leaving the cab driver shouting (I can only assume) obscenities at me. While driving the last few kilometres I opened up the glove box, which he obviously used to keep his takings in, pocketed the cash and completed my journey. I drove the cab to the far end of the drop off point, assuming it would be quieter there and got out of the vehicle.

Before I'd had a chance to retrieve my carrier bags from the back seat, I saw a policeman stood a short distance away, pointing a gun at me. I couldn't believe my eyes, this really did take me by total surprise, as it couldn't have been more than ten minutes or so since I'd left the cabbie by the roadside, somehow he had managed to raise the alarm within that time.

As I was at the end of the terminal building, I sprinted down the side of the building towards the rear. I'd covered no more than 50 metres or so, when I spotted another policeman in front of me, also with a handgun trained on me. I looked behind me, the first officer who had given chase had now been joined by several colleagues, they all screamed at me to get down. Realising I had no option, I sank to my knees, they quickly surrounded me and one of them cracked me an almighty wallop around the back of my head with his handgun. I assume he was trying to knock me out, attempting to make my arrest as easy as possible for them. However, the pistol whip was hard enough to knock me face down into the grass, but I was still conscious and as he'd struck me, his gun had fallen from his hand onto the grass inches from my hand. I instinctively grabbed it, pointed it upwards and let three shots off into the air. I got myself up, looked around and the police were scattering away as quick as their feet would allow. I think it immediately struck me at that moment, as to how powerful a firearm really is; one moment I'm in an almost impossible situation, the next I'm up and running again.

I sprinted away and found some cover behind some small industrial buildings. I got myself into a position where I could see any approach. There was plenty of activity with Police cars and vans flying about, but so far so good. I couldn't stay here for ever and obviously, there was no way on God's earth that I could possibly hope to board a plane, so decided I had to try and make a break for it and get away from the airport entirely.

I picked my moment carefully and made off in the opposite direction of the main airport buildings, assuming that sooner or later I would reach the perimeter fence of the airport and away from immediate chance of arrest. This didn't go to plan and I soon came across a Police Landrover, they spotted me and headed in my direction. I fired two shots, aiming for the front tyre and the vehicle came to a halt. I'd been successful in hitting the nearside front tyre and I used this opportunity to put some distance between myself and them. They had scrambled out of the back door of the disabled vehicle and took cover. This allowed me to escape from their field of vision again.

By now, night was approaching and as darkness came, I felt a little safer. It had also started to rain, although this made things somewhat uncomfortable for me, I think it improved my chances, being more difficult for the police dogs to get a nose on my scent. I spent the entire night undercover, shifting only when I thought I could hear any possible signs of approach. I considered trying to get away several times during the night but (even though the night would give me some cover) the general hubbub of the airport had now died down and there were far fewer passengers around and it just didn't feel right, so I dismissed the idea, thinking I would blend in better when there was more activity in the morning.

As morning broke, from my current position under a bush, I noticed that a bus was arriving and stopping every ten minutes or so, on a section of road about 70 metres away. These buses were generally pretty full and the majority were getting off at this stop and being replaced by a queue which had gathered during the time between buses. I watched until I could see the next bus approaching and made my move. I had noticed there was a decent sized queue waiting to board and hoped I could lose myself amongst them.

I scrambled out from my hiding place, quickly dusting myself off in an attempt to make myself look half respectable as the long wet night had taken it's toll on my appearance. As I made my way in the direction of the bus stop, a building came into my eye line with some men sitting outside, getting closer it became apparent that they were in fact, Policemen and more importantly, Policemen with guns! My mind was in turmoil,

"Do I proceed and take the chance, or retreat back to the relative safety of my hideout and wait for a better opportunity?"

I decided to go back, reckoning my dishevelled state would make me stick out like a sore thumb amongst the much smarter travellers in the queue and I'd be sure to arouse their suspicion, so back I went, hoping another opportunity wouldn't be too far behind.

Fortunately my hopes were realised about twenty minutes later, when a refrigerated lorry stopped almost alongside my bush, the driver jumped from the cab and went to the front of the vehicle. I think he was checking his lights or something similar. This was my chance, the vehicle being so close to my hideout gave me some cover as I jumped out and ran the 10 yards or so to the back of the vehicle, pulled the large chrome handle to open the door to the fridge compartment and I was in! I pulled the door too, making sure it didn't close fully, I didn't fancy the prospect of freezing myself solid. Within a few seconds, I heard the driver's door close and the lorry moved off. It could have only been a couple of minutes later when the lorry came to an abrupt halt, pushing the door open further I could hear the driver coming around the side of the vehicle. I quickly nipped out and ran to the opposite side of the lorry, I heard the fridge door slam shut. I think there must have been a warning light on the dashboard, alerting him of the door being open. As he returned to re-enter the driver's door, I appeared alongside him and using my very best sign language, begged a lift out of the airport. He was very accommodating and took me straight out through the barrier at the perimeter fence surrounding the airport. They had obviously assumed I was the driver's mate and waved the lorry through without a check.

Against all the odds, I'd managed to get away from the immediate danger, but I was still in a foreign country, a long way from Basingstoke. Fortunately the lorry was heading back towards the central Amsterdam area and I didn't complain when he pulled up and gestured to me that I should get out. It wasn't in the centre of the city as it looked semi-rural, but I was in no position to moan. I gave him a bit of cash from the taxi-driver's takings that I'd stolen and he was as pleased as punch.

Other than knowing that I had to get into the centre of Amsterdam to have any real chance of getting away, I had no real idea of my next move at that stage, but one thing was certain in my mind; I was looking like a tramp in my soaking wet, muddy clothes, if I didn't do something before I got into the city, I'd soon be spotted, as the city would be starting to come to life now and would soon be milling with people.I walked a while and came alongside a building site that was still deserted. An idea sprung into my head.

"If I could get hold of a hard hat and high visibility jacket, my unkempt appearance would go unnoticed", so it took no real effort to shin the fence and have a scout around. Within minutes I'd found exactly what I was looking for hanging on some scaffolding, I quickly put them on and made my way back out over the fence. My appearance now wouldn't arouse too much suspicion, I looked like a labourer on his way to work. I walked on hoping to find some inspiration as to my next move. Judging by the road signs, the city was still some way off and I couldn't afford to take my time, the sooner I was on my way properly, the better.

Now, anyone who knows Amsterdam, knows that it's a city of cycles. They are literally everywhere and even here in the suburbs, there seemed to be no shortage. Within minutes I'd found one unlocked and set off towards the metropolis. The journey into the centre of the city took no more than thirty minutes or so and I abandoned the bike in a side street no more than a few hundred yards from the main station. I finished the remainder of the journey on foot. A couple of Police vehicles had passed me on my cycle journey, but my disguise seemed to be having the desired effect; a building worker cycling to work.

Arriving at the station, I made enquiries concerning the journey back to the UK via sea and was told to get onto a train to the Hook of Holland, where I could board a ferry to Harwich. I purchased a ticket and boarded the train, still wearing my hard hat and high vis. jacket.

Within ten minutes or so, the train was on the move.. I gave a huge sigh of relief, I'd managed to get away from Amsterdam at least. The next hurdle would be boarding the ferry, I felt certain that by now the major exit routes from Holland would be on full alert, but I couldn't just give up, I had to give it my best shot.

I'd been told that the train journey would take just short of two hours, but after an hour or so the train came to an abrupt stop. My fellow passengers all seemed to look concerned, making me feel that this wasn't the usual scenario during this journey. I opened a window and peered along the track...there were Police everywhere, but they seemed more concerned with what was going on outside rather than boarding the train. I stayed at the window and bided my time, if they began to board the train I'd have to make run for it, but so far so good.

Around five minutes passed, until a guard passed along the train bellowing an instruction in Dutch, which obviously I didn't understand. Not wanting to alert anyone to the fact that I was English, I said nothing. Just then everybody started to collect their belongings and leave the train, I followed and on alighting I saw that a huge landfall had come down onto the track blocking the rails. (I found out later, this was due to the torrential rain during the night, which I didn't need reminding of, as I'd spent the night out in it!) I followed my fellow passengers and we were herded onto a bus (one of a small fleet) to complete our journey. An hour or so later and we had arrived at the sea port. Now for the tricky part, how do I get onto the ferry?

I made my way tentatively towards the boarding gate onto the ship to figure out what I was up against. At the gate, alongside several customs men checking passports and tickets was an armed policeman. There was no way I could board the ship legitimately with this measure of security, I had to find another way on. I began to have a mooch about for inspiration. I noticed several porters and workmen coming and going, maybe I could pass as one of them, I still had my hard hat and high vis. jacket on, as did they. I saw one of these workers park up a sack barrow alongside a wall and enter a door nearby. Thinking on my feet, I took the barrow and walking confidently strode up to the boarding gate. Giving the officials a nod and a smile, I strode through completely unchallenged! I boarded the ferry, found a secluded corner and hid the barrow, hard hat and high vis. jacket, then casually took a seat as any normal passenger would.

I was obviously worried throughout the crossing that somehow I'd be discovered and arrested, but tried my best to look as relaxed as possible. However, the crossing passed without event and as the announcement came over the P.A. system that we were soon to arrive in the UK, I went back to retrieve my 'workman kit' from my hiding place. I tucked myself away out of sight and as the passengers began to debark, I donned my 'workman outfit' and came out pushing my sack barrow, now loaded with a large box I'd found nearby.

Now came the final hurdle, getting back through immigration and customs! How was I going to manage this? As I followed the masses towards the gate, I could feel the sweat forming on my top lip. Trying my best to look as nonchalant as possible, I began to whistle a cheery tune. As the passengers passed through and had their documents checked, I strode through without a glance from any of them. I'd made it! Somehow I'd managed to get away from Amsterdam, somehow I'd managed to board the ferry at the Hook of Holland and somehow I'd managed to get through immigration at Harwich. The chances of this happening must have been astronomical, but against all the odds I'd done it.

I completed this incredible journey back home to Basingstoke in a rather more relaxed mood and was greeted by Wendy, somewhat surprised I was back so soon. Using a tale of having my suitcase containing my clothes stolen from the hotel, I'd managed to explain my early return AND lack of baggage in one go. She obviously believed my tale because no more was mentioned.

CHAPTER FIFTEEN
THE ROBBERY

After the mayhem of the Amsterdam trip, I was obviously expecting some sort of comeback, so I kept a somewhat low profile for a week or so. However, absolutely nothing happened and I've no real idea why. Surely they must have had something on me, after all I'd left my bag in the back of the taxi I'd stolen to get to the airport. Whatever the reason, I wasn't about to question why I hadn't been arrested, so I drifted back to my bits of skullduggery with Sharon.

We carried on as before, with the 'kiting' and the 'Tweedle' scams. While out in Reading with her one day, we came across a Gunmakers shop, I stopped to admire the merchandise and suddenly the thought of using a firearm in my activities came to me. Why this suddenly hit me I've no idea, maybe the episode in Amsterdam had left a thought in my mind. I'd probably carried out almost every sort of thieving during my criminal career and had progressed to major robberies, involving explosives as mentioned previously, but armed bank robbery had never entered the equation...until now. Without attempting to use this as an excuse, I feel that the concoction of drugs (the strong opiates I was taking to kill the pain in my back and the Valium) had some bearing on my thinking at that time. Whether it was making me more reckless I couldn't be sure, but over the years since, this has always struck me as the most obvious factor behind my sudden change in criminal mindset.

While looking at the guns in the window, I made several mental notes on the shop's layout, looking for potential weaknesses that could possibly be exploited. I reasoned that it would be safer to steal a gun rather than buy from underworld connections, reckoning that the fewer people that knew I had the gun the better. I felt I could get into the shop without too many problems and resolved to return.

I drove back down to the store late one evening about a week later and sat in the car at a distance that was close enough to see what was happening, but far enough away to not look suspicious. The shop closed at 6pm and the staff left some twenty minutes later. I gave it another half an hour, it was now getting dark, I thought it was now safe to go ahead. I managed to get in easily (years of burglary and shop-breaking paid off here) and took an old shotgun and two handguns, a .22 and a snub nosed Beretta. I was now set up to rob a bank.

I drove back to Basingstoke and hid the guns away in my garage, as I obviously didn't want Wendy having any knowledge of them. A day or two later, I was alone indoors and used this opportunity to saw off the barrels of the shotgun, as it was an eighty year old weapon and was about 3 foot long, far too long to be able to hide under my clothing.

In those days, as weird as it may seem, shotgun cartridges could be bought over the counter and I purchased these from a gun shop in Guildford.. I then set about sorting out a disguise of sorts, I purchased a long black wig and a hat in Woolworths and tried them on in front of my wife's dressing table mirror. I looked a complete idiot but totally different from my usual appearance, so felt this gave me the best possible chance of avoiding being recognised. I was so well known to the Police, if a witness gave my description to them, they would be knocking at my door in no time.

Other than taking this precaution, the whole robbery was pretty much unplanned and totally reckless on my part. I woke up one day and decided this would be the day,

it was the 10th November 1976. I still had no idea which bank, or where. Any professional armed robber reading this would probably determine that such a slapdash and unplanned farce would be doomed to failure before it was started. With hindsight, I can see how ridiculous it all was. I put the shotgun into the boot of my gold coloured Austin Maxi and drove over to a certain young lady friend's house (for obvious reasons, I'll not mention her name). I explained to her what I was up to and got her to make me up, making my skin appear much darker than it's usual fair hue. I put on my wig and hat and set off, still having no idea where to. I drove towards London on the M3 from Basingstoke and upon seeing the turn off for Richmond, made my mind up to head there. As I drove through the town, I noticed a bank on the corner of two roads and decided this would be my target.

As reckless as the whole debacle was, I was not about to use my own car as the getaway vehicle, so drove to nearby Kingston and entered a multi storey car park with the intention of storing my car there and to steal another for the robbery and the immediate time after.

Car security was much poorer back in the 70's and I'd pinched more than enough cars over the years for this not to be an obstacle. An Austin A40 was parked nearby and I was soon in. I transferred the bag I'd used to carry the gun, into the boot of the car and set off for Richmond. During the short drive, I noticed a pair of sunglasses on the dashboard and put them on. On the back seat was a raincoat, I grabbed this as I parked the car in a side-street close to the bank, reckoning that this would be useful to put over my arm to cover the sawn-off shotgun. As I opened the boot to get the gun, I realised I'd stupidly left the discarded, sawn-off barrels in the bag as well. I didn't want these left in the car. Fortunately there was a patch of grassed area with flower beds nearby and the soil was soft enough to be dug, I used the barrels themselves to dig a hole and noticing a bag of gathered up leaves nearby, which I emptied, placed the barrels into the bag and tossed it into the hole, pushed the soil back in and scattered the leaves over the area.

It was now 12.30pm as I approached the bank, my heart pounding heavily in my chest. I pushed open the double doors and entered. A few customers were being served, but it was far from busy. I approached a vacant window being manned by a young girl, pulled the shotgun from the cover of the raincoat and raised it where it could be seen, demanding money from the bank teller. She looked horrified, then bent down, presumably to get the cash. I seemed to be standing there for ages and by now everybody in the bank was aware of what was occurring. This period of time was probably no more than thirty seconds or so, however it seemed to be so much longer. All I could hear was the rustling of paper, but the young lady was still ducked down below the counter. I was continually scanning the doors to the street, realising that the longer this went on, the greater the chance of being caught. I stepped forward, to yell "hurry up," I banged the gun on the glass security screen and.....bang....the gun went off. I was shocked, obviously not expecting this I was sent backwards a couple of yards by the kick of the gun as I had not taken a stance to counteract this. The glass shattered and I heard a scream.

As I stepped forward again, I noticed some money in the trough below the counter, (these troughs were fairly new then and I'd not seen one before), I grabbed the cash and fled. In the panic and confusion, I dropped the coat I had been using as cover for the gun. I got back to the stolen car and sped off for the car park in Kingston.

During the drive my mind was in turmoil, this was not how it was meant to happen, I had no intention of using the gun. It was meant as no more than a prop., just a means to an end. I parked the A40 back up in the car park, transferred the gun back into my own Maxi and set off back for

Basingstoke. Reckoning there was the possibility of road blocks, I needed to get rid of the shotgun and quickly. I stopped the car at a quiet spot next to the River at Hampton Court and ensuring there were no prying eyes, launched the shotgun into the Thames, as near to the centre of the river as I could manage and continued my journey home. As I drove back along the M3 towards Basingstoke, my Maxi broke down. I managed to get to a phone and call the AA and as I wasn't actually a member at that time, I had to agree to sign up with the patrolman. Fortunately he arrived fairly quickly and managed to get me going again and I completed my journey back to Basingstoke.

I was still on bail at this time for my involvement in the uncut diamonds affair and I had to sign on at Basingstoke Police station that day, so popped in there before returning home. I can't tell you how strange it felt to come straight from an armed robbery to a Police station voluntarily. This took no more than a minute or two and I drove the short distance home.

As I entered my house, Wendy called out to welcome me back home, she was obviously totally unaware of where I'd been and what had occurred. I tucked the money away safe and sat down in the lounge, reliving the events of the day in my head. Try as I might, I just couldn't understand how the gun had gone off when I tapped the security screen. Wendy called out from the kitchen to let me know my dinner was almost ready. I turned the TV on and sat myself at the dining table, just then the news came on and the announcer stated that a young bank clerk had been shot dead during an armed robbery in a bank in Richmond. My jaw fell open as the report continued and I realised this was MY robbery they were talking about. I couldn't quite believe it, I was sure the young girl was still out of sight when I'd banged the gun on the glass. That was why I'd done it, to hurry proceedings up. Wendy came in and put my dinner down in front of me and went back out to the kitchen. I felt totally numb...surely there was some mistake, it couldn't be the same robbery...maybe there'd been some confusion or mix up at the newsroom. I switched channels to hear the same report. There was no mistake, I had shot a young bank teller dead. Throughout my life, I had been a fairly ruthless criminal, but I had never set out with the intention of hurting anyone. Sure, I had little regard to people's possessions, thieving didn't leave me with any guilt at all, right or wrong, that's the way it was. But this, I couldn't quite comprehend, how could I have killed someone? The overpowering sense of guilt I felt at that time I can't explain, however it is stronger now, some thirty-seven years later. If I had been offered the choice of dying that evening as I listened to the news report and that poor young girl's life being restored, I would have jumped at the chance and still would today.

CHAPTER SIXTEEN
THE AFTERMATH

I made up my mind to try to continue on with things as best as I could. My guilt and remorse didn't disappear and maybe I should have given myself up. I'm not going to try and explain, or even defend my actions and many, many times since I've reasoned that this would have been my best choice of action. However, I didn't and there's nothing I can do to change that now.

The condition of my back had not really improved that much and I was still on the drugs prescribed after the accident. Also, I was still taking far more than I was meant to and it was having a detrimental effect on my mental well being. This coupled with my feelings over the robbery outcome, meant that at times my mind was in a total mess.

I had started an affair with the young lady who had applied my make-up and disguise for the robbery, (who, at that time, was the only person who knew of my involvement in it and the subsequent shooting) and while visiting her on one occasion, a friend of hers who was visiting, made her lustful feelings towards me very clear. I thought little of it at the time, however some days later I drove over to see my girlfriend and when I arrived, decided to abandon that visit and call on her pal who lived nearby. I then started a sexual relationship with her as well. The drugs were seriously affecting me and I was becoming increasingly reckless.

My old partner in crime, JA had come back onto the scene and we'd begun to 'work' together again. One evening, he was over from his home in Potters Bar visiting me on a purely social visit, we went to a pub in Basingstoke and as usual, he was hitting the bottle hard. As I've said previously, I was never really a regular boozer and that evening was sticking to soft drinks, however under constant jibing from JA, "have a proper drink, go on", began to join him on the sauce. Sometime towards the end of the evening, he managed to snatch a bottle of scotch from one of the optics behind the bar. How he managed this I can't recall, but we left in my car both drunk, with the bottle of scotch with a tissue in it's neck in place of a cap. I dropped JA off at the station and by now the booze mixed with the drugs were kicking in and I decided to rob a petrol station. I pulled into a street behind it, went onto the forecourt, kicked the door in with ease, I must have made a hell of a racket (mad behaviour down to the drugs again) and made off with their stock of cigarettes.

As I drove away, at some point I realised that I hadn't switched my lights on, I quickly turned them on but I'd been noticed by a Police car, which gave chase. Whilst this chase ensued the bottle of scotch had rolled around and the tissue in the neck had managed to come out, rather than have the whiskey stinking out the car, I slung it out of the window. (Much later, it came to my knowledge that the Police had picked up this Scotch bottle and lit the contents and reported that I had attempted to throw a Molotov cocktail at their vehicle!) I managed to outrun them, but in doing so I had rammed my car into a lamppost. I abandoned the car and made off on foot, leaving around 10,000 cigarettes and the .22 pistol from the gun shop break-in in Reading in the boot. Why the hell was I carrying a gun in my own car? It was as though I was asking to be arrested, (totally reckless behaviour again). Obviously they would now be looking into the origins of the .22 pistol, how long before they link it to the gunshop in Reading?

Now I was on the run and with Wendy still totally unaware of my involvement in the robbery and subsequent young girl's death, I told her I had to go on the missing list for a while for another matter. She was obviously used to my chaotic lifestyle by now and even though a little upset at this situation, wasn't overly put out. Unable to go home, I booked myself into a bed and breakfast place in Slough. I had signed in under a false name, telling the landlady that I was a businessman, carrying out some transactions in the area for a few months. I needed transport that was obviously untraceable, so I stole and rung a brand new Fiat from a main dealer's forecourt, which I was able to use undetected for some time.

I needed cash to live, so was still getting up to bits of villainy to keep my head above water during this time. One night I broke into an house in an affluent area of Slough and as I roamed around inside, I kept coming across large bundles of cash in various drawers and cupboards. This struck me as strange, however that was what I was there for, so I bagged the money and made my way out considerably richer than when I went in. I also took a really nice quality radio. It transpired much later, that the house was owned by a high-ranking Policeman and no cash was actually reported as missing in the crime report, only the radio, which does tend to make me suspicious of where the cash came from! The cash from this job enabled me to keep myself ticking over for a while, but living under these circumstances was proving expensive. I was meeting Wendy a few times a week at pre-arranged locations, to hand her some cash for herself and the kids, it was a stressful time for her as the Police had raided our house on several occasions, however she still had no knowledge of my involvement in the robbery and shooting. At these meetings she'd often ask when I was coming home, that the kids and her were missing me. I tried my best to console her with a vain attempt at reassuring her that it wouldn't be too long before we'd all be back together again. I knew in my heart of hearts that this was bullshit and to be honest, I realised that life would never be the same again. Over the last few weeks there was much media coverage and reports of the robbery and the young bank teller's subsequent death and a £50,000 reward was being offered for the arrest of the perpetrator. A reward of this magnitude certainly loosens people's tongues and as sure as I was that only one person knew of my involvement at that point of time, it still worried me.

A few months of this way of life and money was becoming extremely short again.

I was actually owed money by the Blue Star garage in Hounslow, that I had done some work for a while back and as things were getting desperate, decided to pay them a visit to ask them to settle their debt. Unbeknown to me at that time, the Police had found my original unsettled invoice to the garage on a raid at my house. Subsequently they had spoken to the manager and issued instructions for him to call them immediately if I appeared.

I drove there, parked nearby and tentatively made my way towards the garage. I couldn't see any abnormal activity, so went to the reception area. The manager was behind the counter and as I'd dealt with him previously, I spoke to him and asked if I could have payment for my work. He remembered me and assuring me that they were in a position to pay now, he went off to get my money. I waited a few minutes, then a few more and still no sign of his return. By now I was becoming increasingly worried and decided to bail out. I left the building half expecting to be pounced on as soon as I came out, however saw no sign of any Police. I was still very suspicious though and decided to continue with my plan of totally getting away. I needed the money badly but decided to go with my gut instinct. As I approached my car they came out of nowhere, probably six vehicles containing around fifteen Police officers, most of them armed, some with dogs. They jumped out, I was totally surrounded and with many guns aimed at me was ordered onto the floor. So the game was up, I was arrested. This was January 1977, around two months after the robbery.

I was taken to Richmond Police station and questioned regarding the robbery, at which point I initially denied any involvement in it and I was then put into a cell. All I could think about at that time, was Wendy and the kids. How would they react when they found out that I was to charged with killing someone, as I thought I eventually would be. A thought came to me immediately that if I were dead, I couldn't be convicted. Without further ado, I decided this was the best option. I had no thoughts on saving myself from a potentially long prison sentence, this was done purely with the kids and Wendy in mind. Obviously they would be upset, but life goes on, I felt this might save them from endless heartache.

I removed my belt, placed it around my neck and tied the other end to the peep hole at the top of the door and let myself hang. I must have passed out fairly quickly, as I have no further recollection of the incident. I awoke three days later in hospital with severe chest pains. Apparently the Police had found me in time, released the belt from around my neck and performed CPR on me, then rushed me to hospital. The chest pains were obviously from the CPR chest pumping on my sternum.

Apparently Wendy had been allowed in to see me at some point during my time in Hospital, but I have no memory of this. She had been brought in by my brother and until that time she had absolutely no inkling of my involvement in the robbery. Once I was discharged from hospital, I was taken back to Richmond Police station and questioned further, at which point I admitted my involvement in the robbery. I told them the whole story, exactly as it happened. I told them where I had disposed of the gun and the sawn off barrels, which were recovered as evidence. However, I insisted (then, as I still do to this day) that I had had absolutely no intention of discharging the shotgun at any time. I was charged and appeared briefly in court and was remanded into custody at Brixton Prison to await the trial.

CHAPTER SEVENTEEN
MURDER CHARGE

So here I was again, back in the hell hole of Brixton Prison, where I had served my first sentence almost fifteen years previously. However, this time I was looking at a considerably longer sentence than my first visit. The conditions were somewhat better than my first sentence, but by any stretch of the imagination couldn't be considered ideal.

Even though I wasn't convicted at this time, I was still classed as a Category A prisoner, (Cat 'A') due to the seriousness of the charges and as such the restrictions on visitors was harsh. The only people who were allowed to visit were immediate, close family members and my legal team. Wendy came in several times, but didn't bring the kids in at that stage, as she felt it would upset them too much. Obviously, news travels quickly and apparently it didn't take long for all the knowing looks from neighbours and the local community. Wendy is a strong lady, but it must have got to her. She also said that the kids were getting some stick at school. There's an old saying 'there's nothing crueler than one child to another' and from what I was told, that saying was being proved right. I couldn't expect anything different though and it was all my fault, absolutely no fault of my family.

The Police had initially raided my house while I was on the run after the petrol station robbery, however during this raid, some shotgun cartridges were found in a cupboard under the stairs. Obviously after the robbery, pellets from the cartridge from the gun I used had been recovered and initially the Police thought the ones found in my house were different. However, they were sent off to the manufacturer for further checking and they confirmed that they had mistakenly been labelled incorrectly and they were, in fact, the same.

I now had to prepare for my trial and as I had no real cash at that time, I was awarded legal aid. On a previous case, some years before, I had used a firm of Solicitors called Lamb, Brooks and Bullock and in particular, a solicitor from there, by the name David Webster. He came to see me initially and then recommended a particular barrister who was subsequently allocated to my case.

The Police had put forward all the charges which would be brought to court, these numbered sixteen and were:-

Burglary and Theft.

Assault Occasioning Actual Bodily Harm

Taking and Driving Away a Vehicle without owner's consent.

Having a Firearm with Intent to commit an Indictable offence.

Robbery

Shortening a Shotgun barrel.

Theft.

Burglary and Theft.

Obtaining Property by Deception

Theft.

Murder

I intended to plead guilty to all charges except the Murder charge, to which I was to plead 'Not Guilty', but ''Guilty' to Manslaughter.

The mitigating points in my defence at that time, were my mental state at the time of the robbery, due to the prescribed drugs I was taking and more importantly that I had not intended to fire the shotgun, therefore had not intended to kill or injure the Bank Teller. My barrister visited me on several occasions during the compiling of my defence when these points were constantly discussed and I was hopeful that they would be taken into account. In fact, I had come across an article in the Sunday Times, entitled 'The Hidden Dangers in Everyday Medicines' which brought up several instances where the actual drugs I had been prescribed had brought on some detrimental side effects in a person's mental well being and behaviour. He asked me where this article had come from in quite a stern manner, which surprised me. I explained that we are obviously still allowed newspapers in prison and was quite taken aback that he acted in this way when I presented him with the article. However, he took this article away and I assumed he would act further on this, by maybe contacting my GP for further reports etc. How wrong I was!

I remained in Brixton Prison for just over nine months, until the trial at Court No. 4, the Old Bailey, which started on the 1st November 1977. It was to be heard by Mr. Justice Melford Stevenson. He was a notoriously tough man and had achieved almost 'celebrity' status after many high profile cases including his defence of Ruth Ellis (the last woman to be hanged in the UK) and presiding as judge at the Kray Twins' murder trial.

He was also rather well known for his somewhat controversial statements; when summing up at the Kray Twins trial he was reported to have said,

"The Kray Twins have only spoken the truth twice during this trial. Firstly when they called the prosecuting lawyer a fat slob and secondly, when they accused me of being biased".

His house in Sussex was actually named 'Truncheons' supposedly to represent his authoritarian views.

From the start of the trial, I felt totally let down by my barrister. It almost seemed as though he was putting forward no defence at all. Whenever we had a recess and I had a conversation with him, I repeatedly told him that he really needed to bring up the matter of the drugs and my mental state due to them. But to all intents and purposes, I was totally ignored.

He kept assuring me that everything was in hand, however he seemed determined not to bring the matter up.

I had witnesses on hand to tell the court how my personality had changed since I had been prescribed the drugs, they were never called. I had also asked Wendy if she would tell the court how the drugs had affected me but she felt too frightened, which I can totally understand. I felt as though there were two Lawyers in court and that they were both representing the prosecution. As the trial progressed my mind became more and more in a whirl. Should I get up and speak myself to tell the court these facts that my Lawyer seemed determined to ignore? Once again, under advice from my defence lawyer, I was told this would make matters worse and chose to heed his words. Whether my speaking would have made a difference, no-one can say for definite, but at least the jury would have had all the facts in front of them before they made their decision.

To make matters worse for me, Professor Mant, the coroner attached to the case, made his statement informing the court, that the shot from my gun had entered the bank teller's body in the centre of the chest. This would prove detrimental to me, as it would suggest that she was already sat in an upright position when I tapped the gun on the security glass, rubbishing my claim that I had tapped the glass in an attempt to speed up the handing over of the cash. At a later date, while compiling facts for my defence, I found this to be incorrect. The shot had actually hit the young bank teller in a much higher position on her body and also to one side NOT in the centre, which backs my claim up and that she was actually just rising from a crouching position when the gun fired, showing that I had NOT shot her intentionally.

The case took three days to hear and nothing went my way from start to finish. The judge delivered his summing up at the end, which also done me no favours at all. The jury retired and couldn't agree on a verdict and went back to discuss further. They returned and had now reached a decision. As stated previously, I had pleaded guilty to every charge apart from murder, to which I pleaded not guilty, but guilty of manslaughter. However, I was found guilty of all charges and sentenced to life imprisonment with a recommendation that I serve a minimum of twenty-five years.

As an example of what I mentioned earlier in this chapter concerning Melford Stevenson; after he'd sentenced me to life, the Clerk of the Court piped up with,

"My Lord, you haven't dealt with Mr. Hart's motoring offences".

To which Stevenson shouted

"Endorse his Licence!"

I was going inside for a minimum of twenty-five years and he gives me an endorsement. Unbelievable!

Twenty-five years....those words hit me like a sledgehammer...I went totally numb. I was taken down to the cells below the court in a complete blur and locked in to await my transport to prison. I sat and tried to make some sort of sense of what had just happened; I was still a relatively young man of thirty nine...when I'll be released I'll be at least sixty-four years of age, a year short of claiming my old age pension. My mind could quite get a grasp of this concept. It can't be right....at least sixty-four when I get out, possibly older?

I didn't see how I could possibly spend that amount of time in prison. I had already served several sentences inside which amounted to a good few years in total, but each time I went in I could envisage the time when I'd be released. This time it was different, try as I might I couldn't see twenty-five years into the future. Thoughts of suicide went through my mind again...surely that would be better than this sentence? To be honest, I didn't know what to think, I was all over the place. After what seemed like hours, but was probably much less I was taken upstairs and into the black maria for my journey to begin my life sentence.

CHAPTER EIGHTEEN
LIFE

I was taken from the court to Wandsworth Prison and back to life inside. The first few days inside were spent trying to come to terms with the whole situation, which was still proving difficult. The initial suicidal thoughts had subsided somewhat and now my mind was more set on some sort of appeal against my conviction for murder. I realise that there was only one person who had to answer for all the crimes committed on that day of the bank robbery and that person was me, but I was determined to prove that I DID NOT intentionally kill that poor girl. I was still livid with the incompetency of my lawyer, who totally ignored the main aspects and facts of my defence and I was also upset with myself for not having spoken up in court on these matters, but a murder trial at the Old Bailey is somewhat overwhelming and intimidating to say the least and one should be led by the advice of one's lawyer. I now know better.

Wandsworth prison is a horrible place, and although I don't like giving blanket coverage to the staff who worked there, I found that a good 95% were nasty pieces of work. The daily routine there was very boring and most stressful. If for example you were at another place when it was time for your weekly shower, tough, no way could you complain about not having a shower, you would just have to get on with it. After a couple of weeks you were put on the work list, this meant being taken to the mailbag shop for two or three hours a day. The bags had to be stitched eight stitches to the inch and if any bag was wrongly finished they were scrapped and you wouldn't receive your pay for that bag. On a good week, I might receive around 75p.

These thoughts on an appeal were eating me up, so without trying to ignore them,

I attempted to put them 'on the back burner' in my mind. I knew things weren't going to happen overnight and that the whole thing is a long and laborious process, so I was attempting to be rather more patient. However, that proved to be rather more difficult to do than I would have hoped it to be, I was having difficulty sleeping as my

mind was in absolute turmoil. My case was the first thing I thought of when I woke up and the last thing on my mind before I eventually managed to fall asleep.

However, I tried to settle into the regime of Wandsworth Prison as best I could, but having now been convicted of murder, I was still (and would be for many years) 'Cat A' and what they call 'on the book'. This consisted of being accompanied by two or three screws whenever I was moving around the prison and 'on the book' meant that every movement I made was logged into a book. Whenever I left my wing to move across the yard I was again accompanied by three screws AND a dog handler with a ferocious looking German Shepherd. I was to remain a Category A prisoner for the next ten and a half years.

Wandsworth has always had a strict regime which was accentuated for me with my 'Cat A' status. Upon waking, the cell door would be opened for 'slop out', taking about six minutes then locked in again. Twenty minutes later, opened up for breakfast then locked in again. Half an hour later and it was time for work, unlocked and marched a short distance to the workshop for sewing mailbags. All the inmates working with me were also 'Cat A' as such, we were totally segregated from the rest of the prison.

As previously mentioned, the visiting restrictions while on remand in Brixton were harsh, but now I was in Wandsworth, I was to discover that they were harsher still. At this stage, it was still only close family members who could visit and even they had to fill in a long and very personal form accompanied by a passport style photograph. My mother, father and Wendy duly sent in all the necessary paperwork and shortly after this, I was due a visit. I was really looking forward to seeing my family, but was shocked when my father entered the visiting room alone. I was enraged when he told me that my mother had been refused permission to visit. What possible objection could they have to my elderly mother visiting me? I immediately called the duty officer over and made my grievance clear, obviously there was nothing he could do at that moment, but I was so wound up. Dad and I continued the visit, but I wasn't in the best of moods, after hearing this about Mum. As soon as I could, I made enquiries about this travesty and eventually it was sorted out, however as everything does in the prison service, it took an absolute age to finally get the news that mum would now be allowed to visit. They came up with some pathetic excuse about it being a clerical error, which I'm pretty certain was absolute rubbish. I'm sure they come up with scams like this as another 'punishment'. Once this matter was corrected, I began to settle more and began to accustom myself with my surrounding and fellow inmates.

An inmate, we knew as Frank Jnr. was also on 'Cat A' with me, after having been convicted of an enormous robbery at a Bank of America with another inmate named George.

I had also become friendly with another inmate named Roger and his accomplice, a guy called John, they had been convicted for several bank robberies and were planning an escape attempt and asked me if I'd like to join them. At that early stage of a long sentence stretching in front of you, you're clutching at straws, desperate for any opportunity and this escape seemed a good idea at the time. They had managed to get hold of a security key known as a 'double' from a screw who they had sorted out financially, which should have improved our chances. However, this was thwarted before it came to fruition. I seem to recall the bent screw double-crossed on the deal and the key was discovered. Luckily for me, I wasn't implicated in the attempt, so received no further punishment for my being part of it. I found out some time later that they had turned super grass and suspect that their efforts to bring me in on their escape attempt was an attempt to clobber me too.

Another inmate I had the misfortune to meet at Wandsworth was Archibald Hall. I say misfortune, as I struggle to recall anyone I disliked as much on first impressions. He had been jailed for five murders while working as a butler for members of the British aristocracy. Four of his murder victims were his employers and the fifth, his half-brother. After his conviction, the press labelled him 'The Monster Butler'. He latched onto me during an exercise period and done nothing but boast of his exploits. I did my best to ignore him, but he wouldn't take the hint and carried on and on with his bragging. Fortunately I managed to miss him on subsequent exercise periods, as they were staggered at random times and in random groups. This regime was brought in after Ronnie Biggs' escape from there some years earlier. The authorities thought it would ensure any escape attempt over the wall would be thwarted if inmates had no idea when they would be in the yard.

Wendy visited me several times while I was in Wandsworth and they were all extremely difficult. To see this lovely woman sat in front of me, knowing that she was destined to spend the best part of her life alone, with three kids to support was heartbreaking. After much soul searching, I decided to ask her to divorce me. How could I ask a woman in the prime of her life to wait at least twenty-five years for me. It would be cruel of me to ask that of her. I didn't want to do this, I loved her dearly, she was a fantastic wife and a caring, loving mother to my kids, but I felt it was best in the long run. So after several months, during another difficult visit I brought the matter up. Wendy was already upset, as she was on her previous visits, so when I told her what I thought should happen she broke down. I think that she knew that I didn't really want this (in my heart of hearts) and at that moment in time, neither did she. She insisted that she didn't want to divorce me and that she was happy to stand by me.

"We've had been married for seventeen years and I've stuck by you through other prison sentences, why would I want to end it now?" she reasoned.

I felt comforted by this and to be honest, it's what I wanted to hear, but a nagging doubt stayed in my mind. However, I tried to put it out of my head for the time being.

My time in Wandsworth was obviously depressing, knowing that this was just the start of what looked as though would be a minimum of twenty five years behind bars. Throughout my time there, I can only recall cracking a smile or laughing just a couple of times. One incident involved an inmate convicted of rape, who somebody played a practical joke on one morning. We had been let out for breakfast, which had consisted of some rather sad, fat sausages. His cell mate had put several of these into his pocket and on returning to their cell had deposited them into This guy's pot. The sausages had so little meat in them, they had absorbed the urine in the pot like a sponge and had swelled up to about three times their original size, closely resembling enormous turds. Apparently, while these rubbish quality sausages were absorbing the liquid, they were hissing and he was convinced he had a snake in his pot! The look on his face when he saw them was priceless.

The only other time was on a Sunday afternoon, everybody on my wing had been locked in their cells for some reason, I can't recall why, but I think most were using the opportunity to try to get some sleep. However, a screw who was not known for his good nature, thought it would be amusing to constantly walk up and down on the slate floored landing with hob-nailed boots on! It was making one hell of a racket and was echoing throughout the wing. There was no doubt in my mind that he was doing this purely out of spite as he knew the inmates were trying to sleep. This went on and on, for what seemed like hours, until someone screamed out "Big boots - big cunt". The wing erupted into a mass of laughter. It must have got to the screw though, as he spent the next half an hour unlocking every cell one after the other, asking if it was each occupier who had shouted at him. As if anyone was going to say, "Yes Guvnor, it was me".

I realised when I entered Wandsworth that I wouldn't be there for any great length of time as it was only a holding prison for the likes of 'Cat A' prisoners. As such, I was asked which prison I would prefer to be sent to for the next phase of my sentence. There were no guarantees that this request would be granted, particularly if your conduct was poor or rebellious. There were about eight or nine possible prisons able to take 'Cat A' men at that time and with Long Lartin in Worcestershire being the nearest to London and my family, I requested a move there, not knowing at that time whether this would be granted or not.

My appeal against the conviction for murder was submitted and I know had to wait until it came to court, I had no real idea how long this would be, but I was determined to try show that I had not shot the young bank teller intentionally.

While I awaited my move, I had a lot of time to think. Throughout my previous sentences, I think I just looked upon my time there as a minor distraction from my life of crime, an interruption to my activities. I don't think for one moment, the thought of going straight had ever entered my head. I suppose I had just accepted my previous sentences as an occupational hazard, something that happened occasionally, that was unpleasant, but just 'one of those things'. Almost the same as straight goers looked upon paying their income tax!

But sitting in my cell in the darkness of night in Wandsworth, my thought process had changed considerably. I was thirty nine years of age and unless some miracle occurred and an appeal was upheld, I would be sixty four years of age upon release...one year before claiming my old age pension. Somehow I just couldn't quite equate that thought, I had always kept myself pretty fit and at thirty nine, I think I could have passed for around seven or eight years younger, but to be released at sixty four, whichever way you looked at it, I would be an old man. I had many a sleepless night with these thoughts bouncing around in my head, to the point of sheer panic sometimes. I felt like screaming out of frustration, it's hard to explain in mere words, there was just a feeling of wanting to do something about my situation, whereas realistically, there was nothing that I could do.

The only thing that was clear in my head at that time, was the fact that my career as a criminal was over. There was no way that I could pick up with my activities at sixty four years of age and what was even clearer was that no way would I want to. After release from a sentence for murder, one is generally on licence for the rest of one's life and the slightest misdemeanour would mean straight back inside.

Crime had totally destroyed my life. Prior to this sentence, I had been sentenced to a total of just short of fifteen years,(actually it was much more, but these were served as concurrent) of which I had actually served just over eight years. Now I had been sentenced to 'Life and a total of seventy three years' (to be served concurrent) with a recommendation of a minimum of twenty five, taking the total of time inside to thirty three years, more than half my age would likely be upon release.

Ultimately, I realise the responsibility for my predicament fell down to me, however I was now beginning to realise how much my somewhat unusual childhood had shaped my life. When I began thieving at eight years of age, I should have been punished by my family, I wasn't....I was actively encouraged (as previously discussed).

I'm sure if everybody thinks back to their childhood, we all have some memory of a slight misdemeanour of some sort. Whether it's pinching sixpence from Mum's purse or a penny sweet from the local shop, most of us are probably guilty of something similar. However, sensible parents would put an immediate stop to this upon discovery. I was sent back for more!

How can an eight year old be expected to learn right from wrong under those circumstances. Sure, I had plenty of time to put things right, I hear you say...and you're right, I did. Just maybe it was all too late by then, maybe it was so ingrained in me it had become second nature. I'm sure criminal psychologists could spend their entire career and more analysing me and still be baffled at the end!

CHAPTER NINETEEN
LONG LARTIN AND THE APPEAL

I was at work in the workshop in Wandsworth when I was taken out, back to my cell to pick up my kit and put into the 'Cat A' van for my move. It was the summer of 1978 and fortunately they had taken some notice of my request and I was to be taken to Long Lartin. This is the way these things happen in prison, you're never told in advance...up, out and gone. This way the other inmates supposedly don't know where you've been taken, although eventually they always find out through the prison grapevine. The 'Cat A' van journey at least breaks the monotony of prison routine and let's one have a bit of a sense of the outside world. I was accompanied (handcuffed) by two screws with two Police motorbike outriders. On the journey I had a strange feeling as I looked out through the windows. Here I was incarcerated for the foreseeable future and outside life was going on, people just going about their everyday business, living their humdrum, normal lives. Whereas for me that had all stopped, life for me seemed as though it was on hold, as though somebody had hit the pause button. They were probably moaning about their jobs, the rainy weather, trivial things. How I longed for their ordinary existence, their nine to five jobs, the miserable rainy weather. As much as I was enjoying seeing the outside world, it kind of brought it all into a depressing reality. It made me ask myself several questions, how much things would things change while I'm away? All my kids would be well into their adult lives by then. My dear wife Wendy would be an old lady by then, exactly the same as I'll be an old man. How would my health hold up throughout my sentence? Before I could make myself anymore depressed than I was already feeling, the journey was over and we arrived at Long Lartin Prison in Worcestershire for the continuation of my sentence. The van drove through the main prison gates and right up to an annexe just inside the gate. I was taken from the van and escorted into the annexe and the first thing I noticed that was different from other prisons was the total lack of keys. There were intercom boxes and CCTV cameras at every door and the screw requested each door to be opened which were controlled by an office manning the monitors and releases on the doors, which slid open automatically. I passed through the reception system which was pretty much the same routine as other prisons and was allocated to my cell and tried to settle down as best as I could. After a few weeks there it all became pretty much the same as everywhere else. I was obviously still on 'Cat A' and as such, the security around me was as tight as ever. Shortly after my arrival, something happened that could have put me into real jeopardy. An inmate, let's just call him Phil, who was in a cell next to mine, mentioned to me just as we were being shown back to our cells after exercise, that he'd put something under my pillow and said for me to look after it for a while. Now, he said this to me, literally JUST as we were going back, so there was no time for me to ask what it was or for me to say no. I went back to me cell and the door was locked. I looked under my pillow to find a large lump of cannabis resin. I was due a search imminently and to be found with a lump this size would have me branded a dealer. Fortunately I managed to let him have it back before anything happened and I let him know I wasn't happy about what he'd done.

After around nine months there I was woken early one morning and taken to the prison reception. Baffled by this, I enquired as to what was occurring, to be told I was being taken to the appeal court at the Royal Courts of Justice in the Strand, London. I had not been informed of my appeal hearing earlier, ensuring I would be unable to inform any friends or accomplices on the outside of my journey and arrange an escape attempt. Around this time, there had been several escapes from prison vans following attacks by armed gangs and with me being a Cat A prisoner, they obviously considered this a real possibility.

This news that my appeal was to be heard lightened my mood slightly, in that there was a glimmer of hope that the murder charge could be dropped, in favour of the lesser charge of manslaughter.

Having never been the subject of an appeal court hearing, my mind was racing throughout the journey to London. What should I say? How should I say it?

I need not have worried too much, as I wasn't allowed to say a word in court! The appeal court hearing was totally between the Judges and the defence and prosecution councils, I was not included at all! The Judges presiding over my appeal were Lord Widgery, Lord Justice Eveleigh and Mr. Justice Smith. Once again, I had the same defence lawyer as at my trial and Mr David Webster represented me and Mr Corkery and Mr. Barby for the crown.

I was totally unhappy with what my council had prepared as the grounds of my appeal. So much relevant content had been omitted. The grounds of appeal they had submitted were unknown to me before the actual hearing, so I hadn't had any opportunity to add points that I considered important. However, at the end of the hearing, the main judge ruled that intent to kill had not been proven.

The definition of murder is; the unlawful killing of a human being with malice aforethought, which basically means that someone has to intend to kill before the act actually happens.

The court adjourned and I was taken back to Long Lartin with a Police escort in front and behind the security van. The Prison Officer to who I had been handcuffed throughout both journeys and the hearing, mentioned to me during the trip back that (due to the judge's statement that intent to kill was not proven) he was fairly certain that my conviction for murder would be changed to one of manslaughter and to be honest, I was thinking along the same lines now.

For this period following the hearing, my mood had improved considerably as I was genuinely anticipating my conviction being changed to manslaughter. If this was to be the case, I was certain that the Life Sentence would remain, but that the recommendation of a minimum of twenty-five years would be dropped.

Two weeks after the hearing, I was transported back to the appeal court, once again in the high security vehicle with Police escorts in front and behind. I was in a fairly upbeat mood, certain that justice would be done, the truth will out and that there was no murder, it had been a horrible accident as I'd always maintained.

To my absolute horror, the finding of the court was that the murder conviction would stand. I was totally devastated and felt that the ground beneath my feet had been taken away. This was a massive blow and I sunk into a major depression. All my hopes had been crushed totally. How could they say that there was no proof of intent to kill, yet still conclude that it was murder?

For months after the decision, my head was in bits. The injustice of it was always uppermost in my mind, I couldn't sleep, it was eating me up. It brought back to me a quote I had once seen written, by Lord Justice Matthew, "Justice is open to all, just like The Ritz Hotel". I felt that I had to do something else to show them they were wrong and with this in mind, I decided to petition the Home Secretary.

This had to be done correctly, so I spent every moment I could, in preparing the facts and necessary paperwork to the best of my ability.

The basis of my petition was that I was wrongly convicted of murder because my council had not put forward a proper appeal, which amounted to wrongly excluded evidence, which should definitely have been included.

This evidence was:-

At the time of the offence, I was suffering from stress and anxiety, which was backed up by a Mr. J.S. Lyon, Consultant Psychiatrist at Basingstoke Hospital. I was taking two different prescribed drugs at the time of the offence, Distalgesic and Valium, each one having adverse side effects. I also submitted the article I had seen in the Sunday Times entitled 'The Hidden Dangers in Everyday Medicine. Distalgesic contains a drug, which may impair mental and physical activity. On Valium, it says it has a direct effect on skill and co-ordination.

My Consultant Psychiatrist at the time of the offence was Dr. Guy Edwards of South Hants. Hospital and he states "There are many variables involved; these are related to the drug, the recipient, psychological and social factors. These would all have to be gone into in a detailed medical-legal way". This was not done and for myself on such a serious charge it should have been included in evidence. My legal team did not even consult my GP before the trial. My GP was the only person who really knew my full medical history. Surely this was vital evidence and should not have been excluded.

The Crown's chief prosecution witness, Professor Mant did a reconstruction of the crime and his photographic evidence had been shown in court. In one of the photographs, he positions himself behind the bank till. He claims to be the same height of the young girl who was shot. He stated in evidence that this was the position the young girl was in when the shotgun was discharged. The photograph shows the hole in the protective screen which lines up with his midriff, which indicates that the bank teller was in that same position when the shotgun was discharged, hitting her in the midriff. A vitally important piece of evidence was not pointed out to the court in respect of this. In another photograph, it shows the young girl in the mortuary and the main injury caused by the shotgun is high up to the right side of her chest, about twelve inches higher than her midriff. As far as I can see, this proves Professor Mant wrong. He also said in evidence that the young girl was standing when the shot hit her. Yet looking at the mortuary photograph it is quite easy to see that she could not possibly have been standing when the shot hit her. It is much more likely that she was just returning from a squatting or bending position when she was hit. Surely this made my version of events much more probable.

In my evidence at the original trial, I said that I thrust the gun at the screen in a moment of impatience, when I saw nobody behind the screen. If the bank teller was just beginning to return to an upright position when the shotgun discharged, I would not have seen her. In addition to that, Senior Consultant Pathologist R.A. Goodbody M.D. of the Southampton University Hospital examined the documentary evidence and all other relevant statements and his opinion concludes; "In my view these observations indicate that the gun may not have been pointed at the bank teller as she bent over to take the money from the cash drawers the counter. Her injuries are compatible with her having stood up suddenly with her right shoulder towards the glass screen, arms above her waist, at the instant the gun was discharged. The gun could have been held rigidly, pointing upwards at about 20-25 degrees throughout the whole time as described by the defendant in his statement. The relevance of this is that had Mr. Hart had seen the bank teller standing in front of him, he would have just told her to 'hurry up' and not thrust the shotgun at the protective screen as he did to get her attention"

This evidence was available at the time of the trial and was vitally important to my defence but was wrongly excluded.

When the shotgun fired, I said in my statement that I was flabbergasted at what had happened and went numb for a few moments. The prosecution claimed that I was cool and collected and well in control of myself. Had this been the case why did I drop and leave on the floor of the bank a raincoat and a plastic sack? These amounted to two clues that would not have been left if I had been cool and collected as the prosecution described. The defence council never challenged the prosecution theory on this matter. That challenge should have been included. This was another wrongful exclusion of evidence.

A letter written to me by a friend while I was in custody awaiting trial should also have been followed up on. I had given this letter from JA's wife to my legal team before the trial, she should have been called for the defence. The nature of this letter tells of my change of character when I began taking the prescribed Valium. This was another wrongful exclusion of evidence.

My wife, Wendy was interviewed by Guy Edwards, Consultant Psychiatrist at Knowledge Hospital, Fareham before my trial. She told him that she noticed a big change in my behaviour when I started taking the prescribed drugs. Her evidence would have been very important to my defence had she been called. This evidence was wrongly excluded. My council had failed to tell the court about my illness and medication at the time of the robbery. Had the jury known that I was not a perfectly healthy man but a man who was under a lot of pressure, stressed out and very anxious, they could well have concluded with the added pressure of robbing a bank on my own an accident was much more likely and that a conviction for murder would not have been safe.

I think the basis of my petition demonstrates how I felt that my legal representatives had totally let me down at my trial. There were so many points that I feel should have been brought up at the trial (AND subsequent appeal), but no matter how many times I had pleaded with them to do so, they chose to ignore me. They assured me that it was all in hand and I just let it go. I'd obviously had many dealings with courts in my past, but not of such a serious nature, so felt compelled to take their advice. I was hoping that bringing these other aspects of evidence to the notice of the Home Secretary, would make them see the injustice of my trial and appeal court hearing.

Once everything was prepared to my satisfaction, the petition was sent off. I expected a long wait for a response, however within three weeks a letter arrived from the Home Office.

When I was given the envelope, I took it back to my cell before opening it. Once safely in the solitude of my cell, I opened the letter with trembling fingers. My heart sunk immediately, it was nothing more than a cursory note stating that they were unable to change the sentence of the court. It was quite obvious to me, that the Home Office did not want anything to do with the legality of wrongful convictions for murder.

The wording of their letter proved to me that they hadn't even read the petition thoroughly. They had stated "they were unable to change the sentence of the court". My petition wasn't concerning my SENTENCE, my petition was concerning my CONVICTION, totally different things.

I had spent countless hours in the preparation of my petition and they hadn't even read it properly. A lowly civil service clerk had probably taken no more than a couple of minutes to give it a quick scan and another couple of minutes to type a rebuttal!

I couldn't leave it like this, I had to let them know their error, so I decided a second petition was in order. This petition obviously did not take so long to put together as all the necessary facts had been included in the first, it was just a matter of pointing out their mistake of referring to my SENTENCE, whereas the whole petition was about my wrongful CONVICTION for murder.

I received a reply in equally quick time as the first and equally as useless too. It made no real reference to the points I raised, just that they could do no more.

Around this period of time, there had been several wrongful convictions for murder and the Government had formed a body entitled The Criminal Cases Review Commission (CCRC). I decided that they would now be my next point of contact. I took my time in again collating all the relevant facts, paperwork and wrongly excluded evidence. I also brought up the Home Secretary's error in misunderstanding my petition. This was submitted and I waited...hopefully.

Once again I was disappointed, the reply I received was of no more use to me than any of the previous responses. I replied, urging them to please re-read my petition to no avail.

It was becoming patently clear, that it was only me who had the slightest interest in my case.

CHAPTER TWENTY
FROM BAD COMES GOOD

Back at Long Lartin, over the next few weeks, the reality of my situation was now really beginning to hit home. This was it, for the foreseeable future...I had nothing to work towards, nothing to look forward to. During the lead up to my appeal, all the necessary paperwork etc. had kept my mind busy and occupied and I still had that glimmer of hope that it would all be worthwhile, that I could get people to see that I had no intention of shooting that poor young girl. I sunk into a major depression, which I assume anybody would in this position.

Wendy visited me shortly after and as much as I was pleased to see her, it was a difficult and awkward time for both of us. She had been as positive and upbeat about my appeal as she could have been, mainly in an attempt to keep me in a similar mood, but now that had failed there was no hope. We tried to make conversation, but we both knew the inevitability of what was to come. I could see it in her eyes, she was trying to tell me but couldn't bring herself to say it.

Eventually, she blurted it out, "I think you were right Mick.....I think we have to divorce".

I knew it was coming and I knew it was the right decision, but it still didn't make it easy to take. We both got upset, we still loved one another dearly, but how could a couple possibly make a marriage last under these circumstances. Poor Wendy had already been put through the mill with having to cope on her own throughout my previous sentences, which were short in comparison of this one. She was a similar age to me, in the prime of her life, it just wouldn't be fair on her. We finished her visit with tears, but there would obviously still be some form of contact in the future due to the kids.

My poor kids, they didn't deserve this, what had they done to have to live their most informative years with no father? All sorts of things were going through my mind. Maybe they'd be better off without me anyway? What sort of an influence would I be on them? Maybe they'd have ended up involved in crime themselves, as I had with my parents' influences?

I was severely depressed after my failed appeal and the news of my wife divorcing me really magnified my feelings tenfold. The very next day, as if matters couldn't get any worse, I was visited in my cell by the prison Chaplain who informed me of the devastating news that my dear Mum had died. I was totally numb for a while until the news sunk in. My dear old Mum had always been there for me, never once even mentioning my faults. I know how I've criticised her methods of child care, but I still loved her dearly and now she was gone. She hadn't been ill, so it came as a complete shock. She was seventy three years old and had a severe heart attack from which she never recovered. My Dad was now alone, but he was still in reasonable health for the time being. I made enquiries about the possibility of attending Mum's funeral, but I never really expected to be granted permission. Surprisingly, I was allowed to attend and I was escorted, handcuffed to two screws, with armed Police officers in flak jackets surrounding the graveside. It was hardly a dignified way to attend your mother's funeral, but at least I was there and I was grateful for that. It was a very sad day and as I sat in the church and looked around at a sea of familiar faces, I couldn't help but wonder how many of these people would pass on before I'd be out? I was taken back to prison immediately after the funeral and once again, the feelings of total hopelessness took over me. I was now seriously considering doing away with myself again, what did I have to lose? The only thing I had were my kids and by the time I was due to be released we would be virtual strangers, aside from the occasional visit and how could I guarantee they'd even want to visit me for the whole of my sentence? They may decide that want nothing more to do with me. My eldest daughter Jane was fifteen, David fourteen and Lucy at thirteen. All too young to travel the considerable distance from London unaccompanied and I couldn't expect Wendy to bring them in after our decision to part. She needed to make a fresh start and as much I would have loved it, it just wouldn't be fair to ask her to come in on further visits. With this in mind I made enquiries as to a solution to this problem and I was told to apply to Basingstoke Probation Service. I submitted the necessary paperwork and waited to hear.

Anyway, one disappointment and upset after another began to take it's toll and over the next few days, the idea of suicide seemed to be my main topic of thought. I must have discussed my feelings with my cell mate at some point, because I was taken from my cell by two screws totally out of the blue. Whether a friend had informed the authorities of my frame of mind or whether they had heard our conversation over the intercom in our cell, I don't know, but they were obviously fearful of what I might do. I was first put into another holding cell and it was there that I realised that I wasn't right. I can distinctly remember being in that cell and going over to the small window covered by bars. This window was open and I had the ridiculous notion of pulling the bars apart and escaping. I pulled myself up so my face was level and the cold wind was blowing onto my face, in the distance I could hear the feint noise of children playing, at least I think I could, or perhaps it was my imagination playing tricks on me. Either way, I had this horrible fear that I would never see children (let alone my own children) playing again, that my life in prison would be my total existence from now on. I then had the image of my own kids playing on a beach, splashing and larking around in the sea. I then questioned whether I would ever see the ocean again. The sense of deprivation was overwhelming. After a short while they came to take me to another more secure cell.

I offered no resistance as they led me down to this unit and stripped me naked, before putting me into a bare cell with a built in shelf-like bed with a thin mattress and no blankets. I initially walked around in this cell, not knowing what to do with myself. The overbearing feeling was that I had now lost absolutely everything, my appeal, my wife, my kids, my dear Mum and now I had lost what little freedom I had within the prison itself. The ability to at least leave my cell for meals and exercise and also now I had even lost the dignity of my clothing. I laid myself down on the bed in total despair, curling myself up into the foetal position and cried and cried. I must have eventually stopped, but I had absolutely no idea how long I'd been there.

The only thing I was certain of, was the extreme cold. My whole body was shaking violently, it was that cold. I could see my breath as clouds of steam every time I exhaled. I felt exhausted, extreme cold temperatures use up so much of the body's energy in an attempt to keep the body temperature at normal levels. As much as I had feelings of wanting to die, I think the natural reaction of self preservation takes over and I screamed as loud as I could to get some assistance, but to no avail. I banged on the heavy steel door to try to attract attention. It was that cold, a slight film of frost had formed on the door and I could feel my hands almost sticking to the metal. I was now panicking, I listened intently to see if anyone was approaching... nothing. In total, helpless despair I dropped to my knees and I prayed. I had never been the slightest bit religious, but at that moment the need to pray to God totally overtook me. I prayed that if there was a God, then please could he help me now.

I pleaded, "Surely there must be another way, if there is I want to try. Is it too late for me?"

The tears rolled down my cheeks as I prayed and then suddenly a beautiful feeling of peace and warmth came over me. I stopped shaking, I could still see my breath in the air, but I didn't feel at all cold. After the terrible despairing feelings I'd been having just moments before I now felt at peace. My whole body now felt an almost glowing warmth and I laid back down on the bed at peace with myself.

I know it sounds corny, but at that moment I believe it was God sensing my despair and helping me. This was the moment that I became a born again Christian and remain so to this day. If God can help me in my darkest moment, then he deserves my dedication. I'd already previously made the decision that whatever happened with my appeal and whenever (or, in fact, if) I was finally released from prison, that my criminal ways were over. In fact it was an absolute necessity, as I've mentioned before, I would be on licence for the rest of my life after being convicted for murder and the slightest of misdemeanours would see me back inside again and now this experience convinced me that this decision was correct.

Looking back now, I can see that this period when I became a Christian was the turning point in my life. My whole outlook changed and I could actually see some purpose in life, albeit behind walls and bars. It gave me something to focus on, which one needs in prison. It wasn't just a case of 'What diversion from prison life can I find?', I know,'"Religion, that'll do!' I sincerely believe that God had put me on the right path for a reason. For years I had led a sinful life and now was my chance to pay something back.

I hope I'm not coming across as a 'Happy-Clappy-Halleluia' sort of person, the type that drives you mad at parties trying to preach the

Gospel, because I'm in no way like that. I just feel that I need to express how I feel about religion, how it came about and how it changed me.

My suicidal feelings diminished totally and after several days back in the cell where I had the bad feelings of never seeing children and the sea again, I was back in the main prison. Also, I received some uplifting news regarding my children. The probation service had agreed to bring them in occasionally for visits and this made me feel a lot better. Unfortunately this was somewhat short lived though, as the Officer who had brought the kids to see me, sat in on the visit and it made everybody uncomfortable. After the second visit, we decided not to continue with this arrangement, it just wasn't working, so I stopped seeing the kids for the time being, unsure of when I would see them again. Now this was obviously upsetting, but I took comfort in the fact that at least they WANTED to see me. I tried not to dwell on the matter, telling myself that it was only temporary.

Another upset occurred with relation to visits some time after Mum's death, when my father and brother came on a visit. The routine on visits when checking in at the desk went like so; my file was brought out and the visitor's details checked against the forms in this file.

When they reported to the desk, the first photograph that the officer placed on the desk in front of my family was of my deceased mother. My father was visibly upset and my brother remonstrated with the officer, to be told that he hadn't realised that my mother had died. He found this hard to believe as the officer in question was one of the two who had accompanied me to the funeral. Unbelievable! My father insisted that the photograph be removed from my file immediately.

Aside from these upsets with my kids and the episode with my mum's photo, the authorities could plainly see my change in attitude and mood and were obviously less fearful of me self-harming. I began to attend the

Prison Chapel regularly and read the bible. The Chaplain there at that time was the Reverend Frank Sparks, a very personable gentleman, who I became friends with. I explained to him what had occurred in the secure cell and we spoke at great length on this matter. We discussed the reason for what had happened, he explained that he thought the Holy Spirit had entered my life and that possibly it came to me at my lowest point and from now on my life would head in the other direction. My interest and dedication to my new found faith continued throughout this time and I was confirmed and baptised into the Christian faith in 1981

My whole outlook to my situation changed from this point on. I had always taken great pride in looking after myself and keeping fit, unfortunately this had slipped somewhat as a result of my depression. I now started to run again on a regular basis, covering great distances during training sessions, albeit within the confines of the prison grounds. Harry Roberts who had been jailed back in the 60's for shooting several Policemen often accompanied me on my runs. 'A healthy body makes a healthy mind' they say and I totally agree. I began to enjoy my fitness regime and incorporated my running with regular gym sessions. During one session I met Reggie Kray, who at that time was also well into his personal fitness. I had seen Reg around the prison, he was obviously well known and was therefore difficult to miss, but this was the first occasion we'd spoke. I found him an extremely friendly man and we got on very well. Our friendship was to last for over fifteen years, as you'll see in further chapters, as he was to follow me to two further prisons. Also, around this time at Long Lartin, I looked into the possibility of studying for an Open University Degree. I made some initial enquiries and decided that Sociology seemed a subject that interested me. A large part of sociology was based on criminology, which I thought I had a head start on! I found out that I could not start the course without some lead-in study, so initially I took GCE's in Sociology and also, English Language. I passed these both with flying colours and was making preparations for starting my degree course when I saw a posting on the prison notice board, looking for inmates who were interested in becoming a Braillist. (A highly skilled person who transcribes passages of text, books etc., into Braille for blind people's benefit). I found out that these transcriptions were to be used by blind children and decided that I'd love to do this to help in some way. I applied and waited to hear further. Unfortunately, Mr. Manthorpe who was the Principal of Worcester College for the Blind came back saying that he appreciated our enthusiasm, but the college had exhausted their budget for the necessary further Braille machines and as such the training couldn't go ahead. I didn't want to leave it at that, so suggested to the Governor that myself and a few other inmates interested in this Braillist training (and also the inmates already on the Braille training with the existing machines) could run a Marathon in the prison grounds and get sponsorship to fund the purchase of the machines. The Governor thought it was a great idea and to give our Marathon some credibility decided that as a keen runner himself, he would also take part.

We all managed to get a substantial number of sponsors, actually far beyond our initial expectations and started our run with a lot of enthusiasm. Unfortunately, the Governor started to flag a lot earlier than everybody else. At one point, I was lapping him for the umpteenth time, when he breathlessly gasped,

"Hart....I can't go on....I'm going to have to stop!"

Not wanting anyone to fail and thwart our efforts to raise the required funds, I thought I'd give him a bit of a gee-up.

"Come on you wanker, don't drop out now, those kids are counting on us doing this!"

Probably not the best way to address the prison Governor!

"Oi, less of that Hart, I'm still the Governor".

It worked though, he nigh on sprinted for some considerable time after my little pep-talk!

The necessary funds were raised and our training commenced. I really enjoyed it and loved the challenge of learning something totally new. It wasn't easy, by any stretch of the imagination but I eventually mastered the art. The only frustrating aspect of it was, that although I could transcribe written English to Braille, as I couldn't actually READ Braille, each page had to handed to someone who could, to be proof read as one couldn't see their own mistakes. However, as I progressed my errors became fewer and further in between. I thoroughly enjoyed my work, transcribing newsletters, sections of the Bible as well as other books and such like.

Time seemed to pass quicker when I was occupied and I now had so much going on with my running, my religion and my Braille work that although I could hardly say 'it flew by', I think it seemed to pass more pleasantly than without these distractions.

I had also enrolled in an English course, which covered English Language and Literature and this progressed into what became known as 'The Thursday Group'. I loved these group meetings, we had regular visitors from the Royal Shakespeare Company, where we would discuss their work and their lives. The inmates would also get up and talk of their lives and backgrounds. Two of these visitors who spring to mind are Sheila Hancock and Juliet Stevenson, who I liked immensely. They were both such warm characters and during their talks and sessions of acting out some Shakespeare scenes, I lost myself entirely. I almost forgot I was in prison for an extremely pleasant hour or two. Their talks brought some much needed humour into our lives as well.

On one occasion, Juliet Stevenson, during some demonstration on drama, was on all fours barking like a dog. I think she was trying to be very serious, but everybody else found it hilarious. I can also recall Sheila Hancock telling us of an event that occurred whilst filming a TV commercial attempting to persuade people to give up smoking. She recounted this story and as soon as she'd finished she light up a cigarette. I don't think it struck her straight away what she'd done, as she looked a bit dumbfounded when the room burst into laughter. Once the irony of the situation had sunk in she roared with laughter herself, then told us that unfortunately she had restarted smoking shortly after shooting this commercial!

As part of this 'Thursday Group' we had regular discussions where we would put an idea forward for debate and I think this was where the idea of inmates talking to children and teenagers, to deter them from becoming involved in crime, first came to mind. I was very aware of the fact that my criminal activities had begun at a very early age and I reasoned that if kids could be dissuaded away from crime before it takes a grip on their character, they stood a far greater chance of staying out of prison in their later lives. The vast majority of inmates are re-offenders, it seems to follow that once you're caught up in a life of crime, it's extremely difficult to get away from. These thoughts were constantly in my mind, surely there is a way to use this practically, it was just a matter of how? I was determined to somehow do something with my ideas, however, it wasn't to come to anything until later on in my sentence.

It was now two years since I had seen the kids, although we had kept in regular contact by letter, which was better than nothing. My Jane was now seventeen years old and was courting a young chap who was a couple of years older than her. At her age she was still considered a minor by the authorities, so unable to visit unless accompanied by an 'adult'. With this in mind, she asked me by letter whether I could add her boyfriend onto my visitors list and then he could be the adult to bring all three of my kids in. I thought this was a great idea and submitted the necessary paperwork. Once again, they came up with yet another mindless excuse as to why this wouldn't be possible. They reasoned that I hadn't known this young chap before I was imprisoned, so why would I want him to visit now? They couldn't see the logic that it would facilitate me seeing my children.

It was therefore another year before I was to see them regularly. Once Jane turned eighteen and officially classed as an adult, she began to bring them in frequently and we were all happy to rekindle our relationships. I'd missed them dreadfully and although circumstances were obviously not perfect, we made the best of a bad job.

Seeing the kids regularly helped me a lot and I felt somewhat settled. My Christianity gave me a peace which hadn't been there before and my Braillist work kept my mind occupied, while my fitness endeavours took care of my body.

An inmate named Max was in the cell next door to me and as I'd met him during my time on remand in Brixton, we struck up a kind of friendship. However, there was something about Max, that I couldn't quite put my finger on, but I never really felt fully comfortable in his company. He was a hardened arm robber, but it wasn't this that bothered me, after all I was no saint myself. One day, he shouted out to me from his cell, telling me that he's left something for me on the landing outside. During the evening, I noticed a Cat A van at reception from my call window and wondered who was being moved. When we were unlocked the next morning, I discovered it was Max who'd been ghosted out and that he had left a selection of pots and pans for me. A couple of weeks later, I was upset to find out that he had in fact, turned 'supergrass' and was giving evidence against the brother of Ronnie Knight (Barbara Windsor's husband). So, the strange, gut feeling I'd had about Max proved to be warranted.

However, the pots and pans he left me came in very handy. Myself and a few of the other London lags, had formed a kind of 'supper club' where we would cook up our own food, (a welcome respite from the usual prison slops). Somehow or the other, I found myself nominated as the official cook for our little group, which consisted of myself, George (a notorious gang member), Brian, Micky and a few others. Brian was a big-time cannabis importer and dealer, as was Micky. Brian was serving six years and was arrested following a customs and excise operation. Brian's M.O. was to bring lorry loads of white goods, (washing machines, tumble dryers etc.) into the country with enormous slabs of cannabis resin in the bases of the machines. He told me a funny tale one day concerning his activities in the drug trade. He travelled to Pakistan to finalise a deal on some Paki-Black (Pakistani cannabis resin) and he visited the area in the hills where it was produced. While discussing this deal, they walked through a field and he said he saw the strangest sight. Some goats had got through a fence into the area where the cannabis was and had munched away at some of the blocks. Apparently they were making the strangest noise, while laying on their backs, kicking their legs around!

We had some great evenings at our supper club, as the food was usually accompanied by some decent quality prison hooch, which livened up proceedings. George hired what we called a 'hobbit' to serve our meals, a 'hobbit' was a lackie or gofer, that he paid a fee to, either in cash or tobacco to act as our butler. I felt kind of sorry for the guy, but he was never humiliated or taken advantage of in a malicious way. George always insisted that the 'hobbit' dressed in his best clothes and with highly polished shoes!

Life plodded along inside until mid 1984, by which time I had been at Long Lartin for approximately six years when I was 'ghosted' out to Gartree Prison.

I now had to go through the process of settling into a new environment again. The authorities don't like you to get too settled in any one place during a long sentence, so shift you around now and again. Gartree, at that time was a dispersal prison and as such there were still many inmates who were Cat 'A', like me, so the regime was strict and the security was as high as at Long Lartin.

The prison, situated in Market Harborough, Leicestershire, had opened in 1965 so was relatively modern in layout and there were considerable facilities for education and study. Once again, in an effort to pass time constructively I joined as many groups and activities as I could. I was still very much into my fitness regime there and played badminton as often as possible.

Reg Kray followed me to Gartree after a short while and I was pleased to see him. I had got on well with him in Long Lartin and during our chats he often confided in me that he feared that he would never be let out of the penal system. Reg and his brother Ron had been sentenced with a 'rec.' of a minimum of thirty years (for the well publicised murders of Jack "The Hat" McVitie and George Cornell) and there was no certainty of them being let out then. I suppose he felt that I would understand his predicament, as I was in a similar position, with my 'rec.' minimum of twenty-five years, I had no absolute guarantee that I would be released at this point in time either.

Much has been made of the bond between Reg and his twin brother Ron and I regularly saw evidence of this, as he always spoke fondly of his brother and how much he missed his company. There must also be some truth in the theory that twins have some sort of psychic communication, often Reg would look unsettled and when I asked him why, he'd reply, "something's up with Ron". Somehow he just knew and he'd always be proved right, when news of an incident involving his brother would be relayed to Reg from Broadmoor Hospital. Ron had been committed to Broadmoor as criminally insane and was to remain there until his death.

I think Reg felt guilty in some ways regarding his brother, not in the sense that he could have made a difference to Ron's mental health, but that he wasn't with him. They had spent their lives together until they were split when Ron was committed and now they were apart and it didn't sit right with him. Several times he asked my advice as to whether he should get himself 'nutted off' (feigning insanity), so that he could join his twin once more in Broadmoor. I must admit, I felt as though I was put on the spot somewhat, being asked to give advice on such a life changing option and I passed the buck back to him, saying that he didn't need to make up his mind straight away and that he needed to take his time and think it over.

He never did opt for the 'nutting off' though and aside from the very rare occasions when Reg was taken to Broadmoor on a short visit to see his twin, they were destined to spend the rest of their lives apart. On the whole though, Reg was good company and we spent much time together training as he was very much into his fitness at that time. Boxing was very much his first love from childhood and his work-out routine was centred around the sport. In fact he acted as personal trainer to Charlie Bronson who was an inmate there at the time. Charlie was a fitness fanatic and would spend hours doing press ups and other bodybuilding exercises. Reg's training would push him to the maximum and I'd often spot Charlie in the yard running or doing star jumps or something similar, as I heard Reg shouting from his cell window, "Give me twenty-five....okay.....now another ten".

I kept in contact with Charlie Bronson for many years and still have some letters from him containing his drawings, which have become quite well known, as they've been shown many times in the national press.

An old friend of mine visited quite regularly while I was here and he began to bring in Pauline, a lady friend of his and after a while she began to visit me on her own and we formed a friendship. She didn't come in every time but I was always pleased to see her.

My kids visited at almost every opportunity and I was very grateful. Wendy actually still accompanied the kids on a few visits, even though we were now divorced, but after a while she met a chap and obviously they stopped then.

Unfortunately, Wendy's new relationship was not to last long, as her new man fleeced her financially and scarpered and I really felt for her. She didn't deserve this, that woman was an absolute saint. When the kids came alone to visit on subsequent occasions, I always enquired after Wendy, as I still cared deeply. I had put her into this position and have always felt so guilty for that. I'm also eternally grateful for the fact that my kids and my ex-wife have always believed that I didn't intend to fire the gun on that fateful day. I know that if I hadn't attempted to rob that bank and that if I hadn't taken a firearm, none of it would have happened, but I did and I can't change anything. However, guilty of attempting to rob the bank and guilty of going armed I may be, but I was not guilty of firing the gun intentionally and I would hate to think that my nearest and dearest thought I was.

Gartree was very similar to Long Lartin in many ways, after a while prison just becomes a routine and any little diversion from that boring regime is a welcome break. An incident that springs to mind as an example of this, occurred one day when we were all going about our usual business when an almighty bang interrupted us. Everybody stopped what they were doing immediately and I could see the look of panic on a couple of the screw's faces. Was it a bomb? Several IRA prisoners were here and it wouldn't be beyond the realms of possibility that they could use explosives in a break-out attempt.

After much scurrying about, the real reason for the 'explosion' was revealed. An inmate had been brewing 'hooch' (illegal home-brew prison booze) in the corner of his cell and had sealed the lid on the container too tightly. The pressure had built up and up, until the container couldn't take any more and the whole thing had gone up like a rocket! Potato peel, orange peel, sugar and water are left to ferment for as long as possible to get the strongest possible brew but during this process, it bubbles away and the air bubbles produced need some escape. Unfortunately in this case, our would be master brewer hadn't realised this and paid accordingly. His cell looked as though it had been pebble-dashed, there was crap and muck everywhere. Our wing smelt as though it was a distillery for days afterwards. It was just as well the inmate in question wasn't in the cell at the time, as funny as it was, it wouldn't have been quite so funny for him had he been there.

A couple of other incidents, of a rather more serious nature that occurred during my time at Gartree, also come to mind; I was in a cell on the top landing, where all the Cat A prisoners were placed. In between each Cat A prisoner's cell, an ordinary inmate was housed and every month, (for security reasons) two Cat A men swapped cells. On many occasions, I swapped with a man named Sydney Draper, who was serving life for murder. I had a lot of sympathy for Sydney, he was suffering from stomach cancer and was shown little or no compassion by the prison staff for his situation. Anyway, a group of us, including Syd, were out in the playing field on exercise, when suddenly an almighty roar broke the quiet and a helicopter (which had been hijacked) came roaring over the prison roof and quickly landed. Syd and another inmate, an armed robber by the name of Kendal, sprinted over, jumped in and within seconds the chopper was airborne and away. Even though I was quite close to Syd, I had no idea this was on the cards, but I was quite pleased for him, given his medical condition. Unfortunately Kendal was captured only ten days later, Syd managed to stay on the run for thirteen months.

The other incident occurred on what started as a quiet evening around 6.30pm. The cells were unlocked for association, some inmates opted to use the gymnasium, some attended various courses in the education department, various other inmates carried on with their respective hobbies using small tools which were issued by the wing office, while others, (myself included) decided to watch TV. The documentary I had been keen to see ended and I returned to my cell. As I approached my door, I could see two legs protruding from the doorway opposite mine, it transpired that it was a screw kneeling down. When he heard me approaching, he shouted to me to bring him some scissors. As I handed him the scissors, I looked over his shoulder and immediately wished I hadn't. The inmate allocated to this cell, a guy named Woody, was laying in a pool of blood with his hands tied behind his back. He had been stabbed numerous times with a pair of scissors and was dead. As the screw left the cell to report the incident, he handed me the thick string used to tie Woody's hands together and I entered my cell, threw the string in the waste bin and sat on my bed, shocked at what I'd just witnessed. Woody had been a bit of a loner who kept himself to himself mainly, but was quite well known as he'd been on the wing for many years. Everyone was locked in their cells to await the arrival of the Police, who subsequently questioned all inmates on their whereabouts throughout the evening. The CID Officers I spoke to were already aware of me assisting the screw by getting him the scissors and they took away the contents of my waste bin containing the string used to restrain poor Woody.

An inmate by the name of Fred Lowe was arrested and charged with murder a few days later. He had used the hairdressing scissors that had been signed out to him. Apparently he took the scissors back to the wing office covered in blood. He was asked whether he had cut someone's ear to while replied, "Go and look in Woody's cell". He was eventually convicted of murder and was transferred to Long Lartin prison where he stabbed another inmate to death.

While incidents like this didn't happen every day, violence was always a regular part of prison life and with this fact always in my head, once again the idea of starting some sort of scheme to avert kids away from crime was churning over in my mind. I began to talk to my fellow inmates about this by asking them how they'd feel if their own children followed in their footsteps. Almost everybody, (except the downright stupid) said they would do anything to stop their kids getting involved in criminal activities. On the strength of this, I formed a committee and we met as a debating society on a weekly basis to discuss where we could take this idea. In fact I wrote a paper, entitled 'Prevention not Prison' which was submitted to Lord Justice Woolf.

A very popular, easy going screw called Bob took a great interest in our committee and sat in our meetings and would put his ideas and points of view across to us. I liked Bob and valued his help, he got on with most of the inmates on our committee and liked to feel almost as though he was 'one of the chaps'. One of the lads played a rather cruel practical joke on him one day which, fortunately he took in good part. While we at a meeting one day, Bob was handed a roll-up ciggie, which, unbeknown to him, contained a liberal dose of puff (cannabis). Bob lit up and smoked away, totally oblivious to the constants of his 'rollie', until he tried to stand up afterwards. Poor Bob's legs were like rubber, he was all over the place. He suddenly realised what had occurred, "You bastards" he screamed, "I can't bleeding walk". The committee was in uproar, we told him to sit down and let it pass, we'd hate to see him go downstairs in that state, we joked "you might get nicked and drug tested!" As I said, Bob saw the funny side of the situation and sat down again until he felt his legs were working again.

As in all prisons, drugs were rife and this situation has definitely worsened with time. I managed to avoid almost all personal contact with them, my personal fitness and well-being being my main priority.

My involvement with this committee and my sporting activities all helped to keep my mind off my case. Even though my original appeal had failed during my time at Long Lartin, I was not content to let it stand at that. I was determined to follow this through until I could prove I was not guilty of wilful murder. The fact that the appeal board had shown that 'intent was not proven', yet the murder charge still stood, baffled me. This was something I needed to do, but these things can't be rushed, particularly when you're inside, so any diversion to stop me driving myself mad with the complexities of my case was welcome.

Around this time, I began to take up the craft of woodwork and my passion and interest for this engaging hobby lasted many years. I made some beautiful pieces of small furniture, with inlaid tops of which I am very proud. Small, intricately carved jewellery boxes and ornamental gypsy caravans took up many lonely hours in my cell. I'd often work for hours and hours at a time and when I stopped for a break to have a cup of tea, I'd be amazed at how long I'd been working away, totally wrapped up in my endeavours. I'd always been good with my hands, due to my engineering background, but now I was using these skills more on the creative side and I surprised myself with the results. Many of these gifts were given to friends or sold to supplement my meagre income in prison, but I have kept some to this day and I often look at these pieces and my time in prison comes flooding back to me.

One inmate remains very fixed in my memories from Gartree, a chap named Barry. He'd come from a family in Watford and his parents had split up when he and his brother Glen were young. Their father had emigrated to Australia and became quite wealthy and when he died he had left several provisions for his two boys in his will. The first provision was £100,000 to each boy to start a business, which they both did. Glen's business flourished, but unfortunately Barry's floundered and left him destitute. So depressed by his situation, he rode a motorcycle straight up through the doors of a bank and robbed it! He was captured shortly afterwards and given a lengthy sentence. Barry and I became great friends and we often talked for hours, he was a fascinating character. I always believed that if he hadn't been left the money to start the business, he wouldn't have been in prison, he just didn't seem the type. He hadn't really been in trouble before and it strikes me that going from having £100,000 to nothing drove him to commit the robbery. However, there is a slightly happier ending to this story, in that another provision from his father's will bequeathed him a further £400,000 during his time in Gartree. That lightened his mood somewhat and at least gave him some hope for his return to society. I told him in no uncertain terms to use the money wisely when he got out. £400,000 was and still is, a sizeable amount and should lead to quite a comfortable life, if used sensibly. Barry thanked me and bought me a beautiful Roberts radio that I still own to this day.

Other inmates in Gartree during my time there included several IRA bombers who I used to see around, but really didn't have any dealings with. They tended to keep themselves to themselves and didn't really mix with anyone out of their immediate circle.

Three members of the 'Carl Bridgewater Four' were there also. This was a well publicised case, where a young lad (Carl Bridgewater) was delivering newspapers to a farm when he disturbed burglars and was shot dead. Four men were subsequently arrested, three were found guilty of murder and sentenced to life in prison, while the fourth was found guilty of manslaughter and sentenced to twelve years. Molloy, the man sentenced to the shorter sentence actually died of a heart attack before he was released. The three remaining men, (Jim Robinson and cousins, Michael and Vincent Hickey) protested their innocence from day one and would let anyone within hearing distance in Gartree know that. I didn't know enough about the case at that time to make any personal judgement, however, after almost twenty years in prison, their case was overturned and they were released. Thinking back now, I can sympathise with how they felt, twenty years inside for something you didn't do, must eat away constantly. My case is obviously very different to theirs, but I still feel a similar angst with a need to prove that I did not fire the gun intentionally.

I also became friendly with the 'Birmingham Six' during my time there. They had all been sentenced to Life in 1975 for the well publicised Birmingham pub bombings. They protested their innocence from day one of their sentence and they were finally released in 1991, when it was decided that their convictions were unsafe. They were all awarded compensation ranging from £840,000 to £1.2 million. These were absolutely vast sums, but how can you compensate someone for taking away 16 years of their lives.

Some of the members of the Guildford Four were also there. Their case was somewhat similar to the Birmingham Six and they were also exonerated and released.

An interesting character by the name of Mabrook Al Gidal was also in Gartree during this time. Mabrook had been a lorry driver in Libya and had volunteered to help Col. Gaddafi and the Libyan Government. The Colonel had subsequently arranged for Al Gidal to travel to London and set him up in a flat in Earls Court, with instructions to assassinate a Libyan lawyer living in London. This lawyer was supposedly working for the Libyan Government and his duties were to supply Gaddafi with sensitive information concerning the British Government he was privy to, through his work. However, it had come to Libya's attention that this lawyer was now working as a double agent and in fact, leaking information to the British Government. Al Gidal was supplied with a handgun, shown where the lawyer worked and as per his instructions, shot the double agent dead. He was arrested almost immediately, tried and jailed. He spoke very little English when he'd arrived in the UK, however by the time I encountered him he'd improved his grasp slightly. He managed to tell me a rather amusing story of his time in London before the assassination, when he decided to sample the nightlife in Earls Court. He approached the door of a nightclub to be denied entry with the reason that he was a 'black man'. Undeterred, he continued his tour and approached another nightclub, unfortunately he suffered the same result of being denied entry, this time for being a 'white man'. He was totally baffled, he couldn't get his head round it at all! For all the language problems, I found Mabrook to be a personable man and got on well with him. I told him about my work transcribing documents into

Braille to help the blind and he expressed an interest in learning this art. I told him this would be difficult due to the language problem, but he was a tenacious character was adamant that he wanted to learn. Some four months later, he was helping me transcribing books and other literature into Braille for the blind college. I gave him 100% for effort! This was no mean feat for a man with his obvious disadvantage.

A high profile inmate named Harry had also been moved to Gartree while I was there and I still spoke to him regularly. He had been convicted of shooting three Policemen back in 1966. He had always struck me as a very quiet and reserved man right from when we met in Long Lartin and we enjoyed many a chat. He has recently been back in the news, as he has finally been released after a total of forty-eight years inside. Harry had a little cottage industry going on during his time at Gartree. He had a team of inmates assembling little trinket boxes which, once assembled, Harry decoratively painted the lid. He must have had a real love of canals, as the painting was always a variation of long boats on a canal. Once they were completed these were sold on outside the prison. I always used to joke to him that he would be the only inmate to earn a million while he was inside!

One piece of good fortune at Gartree, was that I was downgraded to a Cat B, which made life more bearable with far less intrusive security measures.

The aforementioned committee continued throughout my time in Gartree and we attempted to progress the scheme further and applied to have youngsters who were on the verge of becoming involved in trouble, come into the prison for a presentation in an attempt to turn them away from crime before they became too involved.

Unfortunately, even though the authorities thought this was a fantastic idea, the request was tuned down flat and our vision of setting up the crime diversion scheme could go no further here at Gartree. However, I still had hopes of doing something with it and continued to discuss potential ideas and theories at the meetings.

The authorities at Gartree allowed us to keep Budgerigars and I had a great big lump called Rudyard, he was the biggest Budgie I'd ever seen and I taught him to say "Rudyard's a big Budgie". I came to regret this, as once he'd learnt to say it, it progressed to "Rudyard's a big, big, big, big, big Budgie" and this went on and on and on, driving me to distraction.

My Christianity continued throughout my time here and I regularly played guitar at services in the chapel. Also, I began to take a real interest in writing music during my time there. I wrote several songs which I performed at services, occasionally accompanied by a Salvation Army band. Sometimes, while practising my guitar playing in my cell, inmates would hear me as they passed, poke their head round the door and ask if I could teach them. I was more than happy to help anyone and this became another enjoyable pastime.

It was now 1991 and I had been in the prison system for fourteen years since my murder conviction. My children were now all into their late twenties, in fact my eldest daughter, Jane coming up to her thirtieth birthday and had given birth to my first granddaughter and first grandson during my time in Gartree. Kate was born early in 1987 and Ian, in early 1989. I hadn't been able to see them by the time I was moved to Maidstone Prison in Kent.

JA's ex-wife, Jean visited me in occasions during my time there and I really felt for her. JA and her had split up some time earlier and she had contracted Multiple Sclerosis and was suffering quite badly. She used to get a taxi from home to the prison to visit me, which used to cost her a fortune, but she insisted she wanted to come and I was very grateful.

My Budgie Rudyard, unfortunately couldn't be taken with me to Maidstone, so my son David took him home where he lived quite happily, until he found him floating in the kitchen sink one day. Poor David was heartbroken!

.

CHAPTER TWENTY TWO
MAIDSTONE

Upon arrival at Maidstone, I obviously continued on my Cat B status and as security measures at Maidstone were more relaxed anyway, it made life bearable.

A prime example; on my first night there a service was taking place in the chapel, which I wanted to attend, so I asked a PO how I could get there. He took me along a corridor, opened a door which led out onto the yard and just pointed in the general direction and left me to my own devices. I couldn't believe it...it was the first time in many years I'd been given such freedom and it felt kind of strange, but very welcome. As I crossed the yard, I noticed that there was only one wall onto the outside. All the Cat A prisons I'd been in previously had a series of fences and walls, so all in all, it as though a great big weight had been lifted off of me. The cells there were far larger than anything else I'd seen during my sentence and had a proper toilet, rather than the time-honoured pee pot.

My first thoughts at that time centred around getting further along with the crime aversion scheme and it seemed a lot more possible here, due to the easier security measures.

I quickly became involved in my church activities here and became part of a ten piece worship band, playing the guitar regularly at services. The Chaplain here was a very nice man called Edward Ginn and when I spoke to him about my thoughts concerning the youth crime diversion scheme, he couldn't have been more enthusiastic.

At last things were beginning to get moving! Obviously, the Police had to be informed of the details and they bent over backwards to do as much as they possibly could to help.

Unfortunately, shortly after my arrival at Maidstone, I had the upsetting news that my eldest brother Peter was in intensive care and unlikely to live for too much longer.

They allowed me to visit him in hospital at Milton Keynes, escorted by five warders and poor Peter was in a terrible state and it was no more than a few hours after my return to prison, that I was informed of his passing. Once again, I was thankful for being allowed to attend his funeral, albeit accompanied by screws. While at the wake, at which I stayed for about an hour and half, I was given drinks which supposedly were glasses of lemonade. The contents of each glass, actually consisted of about 90% Vodka and 10% lemonade. As I've mentioned before, I've never been a great one for the booze, but the buzz of the alcohol numbed my grief at losing my brother. When I finally left the wake, my brother's wife gave me a pair of Peter's braces as a keepsake and when I returned to prison they tried to confiscate them from me. In my drunken state, I kicked up such a fuss and palaver, but they insisted. I ran amok and managed to get away from them for a while, but they managed to eventually get possession of them.

However, they were returned to me some days later, just going to prove that they were only taking them from me in pure spite.

Once things had settled down a bit after Peter's funeral, I set too in earnest preparing songs and testimony speeches from myself and other inmates for the first group of youngsters to come into Maidstone for our 'pilot' crime diversion scheme presentation. Things had progressed significantly and the authorities had agreed to the scheme going ahead on a trial basis. I had been extremely fortunate in securing myself a job in the prison gymnasium in the afternoons and therefore my mornings were free and I was allowed to spend them in the chapel rehearsing for the presentation.

I had prepared my opening introduction speech to the kids, followed by my own story of my early beginnings into a life of petty crime and the serious descent into heavy, hard core misdemeanours, culminating in my present life sentence. I had always felt that kids are led by peer pressure and that it only takes a few steps and a bit of goading from their pals and their life can change almost overnight. I know my own early experiences were not lead by peer pressure but of being encouraged by my parents, however it made stealing feel as normal as kicking a football around in the park. I thought everybody done it!

A conviction can be almost like scoring brownie points to a wayward youngster, something to brag about to their mates, make themselves feel cool. However, they soon find out how very un-cool it is when they get banged up for the first time. The papers love to publish stories of how much like luxury holiday camps modern prisons are and how all inmates have Playstation consoles and wide-screen TV's in their cells. However, they're not so keen in showing stories and pictures of inmates having their faces and bodies slashed with a Stanley knife so badly, that they require over 300 stitches to put them back into one piece, over a matter as trivial as a few roll-up cigarettes.

During my many years in prisons, I've seen men who considered themselves real hard cases, crying like babies after a few days in the prison system. Believe me, it's hard, very hard and this is what I wanted to bring across to the youngsters we'd be talking to. I didn't want to make the thing a horror show, but I wanted it to contain a hard-hitting message; petty crime is just the start of it....it very often leads to much more serious crime and the time to stop....is now, before it's too late.

I've said many times throughout this book, how I felt my dysfunctional family life as a boy started me off as a thief. However, as much as I feel that was wrong, I would hate to think that the reader would get the impression that my Mum and Dad were horrible people, they weren't. Their parenting skills may not have been the best in some respects, but that aside I always had a lot of love and affection from my parents, particularly my mother and as a kid, I was always clean, well fed and cared for.

In our preparations for the presentation, some of my fellow inmates' personal stories made my own upbringing look like a member of the royal family's in comparison. Some of these poor fellas' stories brought tears to my eyes; being sexually and physically abused by their parents, seeing their mothers beaten to a pulp by their fathers, witnessing their mother selling their body for their next heroin fix, was it any wonder these youngsters ended up where they were?

The first visit of the youngsters (to what was officially now known as The Maidstone Prison Youth Project) was well covered by the press and it all went well.

Hugh Bradshaw, the prison governor had been very supportive since he heard of my idea and he obliged us with the use of a PA system and spotlights which were focused on the inmate giving his testimony.

Edward Ginn, the chaplain who I've mentioned previously had also been very instrumental in helping to bring my ideas to fruition.

After my story which seemed to hit home as required, I performed a song called 'From the Heart', which went:-

If you steal something on a whim
And think you've been so smart
It's just the devils way of giving you a start
He'll let you go on to bigger things
Perhaps you'll reach the top
So rich and pleased and proud you'll be

Then he'll let you drop
In a prison cell you'll land
So cold and grey and bare
This is where the pain wont cease
And who do you think will care
Prison is a dreadful place
Where you'll feel the pain
Separated from those you love
And may not see again
But now you'll think of those you love
Those you've put to shame
They'll suffer just as much as you
And it could all be in vain
So take a long look at your life
And see the way you're going
STOP before it's too late now
Or mailbags you'll be sewing
This advice comes from my heart
I care about you all
Pick it up and take it in
And make sure you don't fall.

Some other songs we performed as a group and the youngsters left a lot wiser than when they came in I think! The lyrics of these songs described in full detail all of the indignities and horrors of prison life; the humiliating reception experience of a full strip search and examination, the frightening first night in your cell, intimidation and bullying by other inmates. Compared to how the presentations became, these first few in Maidstone were a little basic, but from little acorns do great oaks grow!

A video was made of one of these meetings, which we entitled 'Behind a Wall' which is still shown to youngsters as part of the scheme. We ripped off the music from Oasis' 'Wonderwall' and added our own lyrics, which I think worked quite well, as the kids related to the familiar tune. The facilities in Maidstone were far superior to many prisons and we were fortunate to have a swimming pool there. As I had trained to be a lifeguard during my time in the army, I put myself up for the job here. The authorities seemed keen on the idea, but opted to put me through another training course to hone up my skills, as it had been a good few years since my time in the Services. As I've mentioned many times, I was always eager to learn new skills, so I took the course enthusiastically. Much of the content I was already familiar with, however I also learnt a few new techniques and I subsequently started my job in the pool.

Sometimes when a newcomer to the prison came into the pool for a swim, they would see me there and assume that I was a PO and ask if it was okay for them to have a dip. Realising their mistake, I'd play along and say "yeah okay, but no messing about or you'll be out!" When they found out my real status, they'd generally take it in good part.

There was a grassed area just outside the pool building and during the warmer weather, I used to sit outside with some of my pals and enjoy the sunshine. My old pal, Reg Kray was now in Maidstone too and was a regular visitor to the pool. We all got on well and spent some great times there.

Less than a year after being at Maidstone, my youngest daughter Lucy, who was now twenty-eight years old gave birth to her first son, followed a few months later by Jack, my eldest daughter Debra's third child. On occasions the authorities allowed a 'family day', where more than the usual number of visitors were allowed in and I was thrilled when Jane brought in her two eldest kids who had been born during my time at Gartree. Kate and Ian were now busy little toddlers and I felt quite the doting grandad. It was a beautiful day and we spent most of it either swimming in the pool or on the grassed area nearby. Later on during my time there, my son David and his wife had a lovely little daughter, Ann and my daughter Lucy gave birth to her second son, Ryan.

After so many years having no other company other than fellow inmates, it was a fantastic feeling to feel almost normal again. To play with my grandchildren and hear their joyful laughter was fantastic. However, it took me back to that dreadful time in that strip down cell when I doubted whether I'd ever hear kids laughter again in my lifetime. I think this brought it home that maybe, there could be light at the end of the tunnel, although there was a lot more tunnel to travel though before I saw that light in it's full brightness!

I had now been in prison on this sentence for approximately sixteen years and although my surroundings were more comfortable than earlier on in my sentence, I was well aware of the time still in front of me. With this in mind, I still continued to engage myself in as many activities as possible. Obviously the crime diversion presentations and their preparations took up a great deal of time and I was still very much into my woodworking endeavours. I never understood how inmates, with long sentences in front of them, are prepared to do as little as possible and just sit in their cells smoking and drinking tea. Surely keeping your mind busy and occupied is favourable, each to their own I suppose, but that wasn't for me.

Tea wasn't the drink of choice for some of the more well connected inmates at Maidstone though. It was amazing the amount of booze that was around in there at that time. One evening a fella poked his head around my cell door to tell me that I had been invited upstairs to see

Reg Kray. I followed him upstairs to a cell, whose cell it was I've no idea, but it definitely wasn't Reg's. The cell was locked from the inside and the other guy tapped on the door, the flap opened and a pair of eyes peered out to see who was there. The door opened and we went in, there was Reg Kray, two other friends of Reg named Fred and Mickey and a couple of other guys. Apparently it was Reg's birthday and laid out on the table was every spirit you could think of, Champagne, mixers, the lot. In addition to the booze, many other 'party ingredients' were on tap! Reg beckoned me to sit, I was handed a drink and told to help myself to anything I wanted. How they managed to get this lot in, I'll never know, it was astonishing. As mentioned previously, I'd never been much of a party animal but I was happy to have a drink or two with them. During the evening, a message blared out over the PA system, telling Reg Kray to report to the main office. Now, by this time, Reg was absolutely messed, so asked me to see him down the stairs safely. I led him out and proceeded down the stairs in front of him, ensuring he didn't fall and as I approached the office, I let him walk the last few yards on his own. Telling him I'd wait for him to take him back upstairs, I watched as he bounced his way the last few paces. I overheard the conversation from my position, Reg opened the door and slurred,
"What is it?"
"There's a phone call for you Reg, it's from America"
"Tell them to call back tomorrow, I'm busy!"
With that, Reg ricocheted his way back to me and I saw him safely back to his birthday party. I couldn't help but chuckle away to myself as I steadied him along. The authorities take a phone call for Reg, from America, call him to the office to allow him to take the call and he has the cheek to tell them to ask the caller to call again tomorrow as he's too busy! Only Reg Kray could do that!

On another occasion in Maidstone, I had a visit from the aforementioned Mickey, who had now been released, accompanied by a striking looking young lady with a shaven head (a la Sinead O'Connor) and I could see that Mickey had already had a few drinks. Reg Kray was also having a visit and was on the table adjacent to mine. We had small plastic cups on our table containing lemonade, which were being constantly topped up from a large plastic, two litre bottle of vodka! How Mickey got that in there, I've no idea and to be honest, he wasn't being too careful about concealing the pouring out either. It seemed that a blind eye was being turned, as long as no real trouble was being caused or any major breach of security occurred, nothing was said. When the visit finished, I'd had a few drinks but Reg was absolutely hammered. His face was scarlet and his nose looked as though it was throbbing, but nothing was said and we were given a very basic tap down search and sent back to our cells. At that time, parcels of clothing etc. were allowed to be brought in and Mickey had been kind enough to bring me in several pairs of good quality training shoes, track suit bottoms and sweatshirts, for which I was very grateful. I subsequently found out that Mickey had ordered these items from a shoplifter friend! Stolen or not, they were far better than wearing the ill fitting rubbish they issue you with in prison. Life continued and the Maidstone Youth Project went from strength to strength. By the time I was moved to Coldingley Prison in 1995, we'd managed to speak to many youngsters and I like to think some of these kids had been persuaded to give serious consideration to their lives. Hopefully if they were heading in the wrong direction, we had managed to convince them otherwise.

I was informed about my move by a very pleasant female PO, who came to my cell to let me know I was on the move soon. They never tell you where you're heading, just that you're going and you don't find out until you get there. I was upset at this news, after working so hard to finally get the Maidstone Youth Project off the ground, from having the initial idea some years before, I was reluctant to leave it behind. I made my thoughts to her very clear, in fact I recall telling her that I wasn't going, which was pretty pointless really. She told me, apologetically "Sorry to have to do this Mick, but you're going and you can go the easy way or the hard way". The easy way was walking out to the van, the hard way was your cell door opening with a bang at around 4 a.m. and eight big warders storming in with a mattress in front of them, flopping it on top of you and then being injected with Mogadon and dragged out to the van. Basically, it's a no-brainer, either way you're going, so there's absolutely no point in making things harder than they need be. Realising this I held my hands up, reluctantly.

CHAPTER TWENTY THREE
COLDINGLEY

As I sat on that van for my transfer to wherever, I felt saddened that all my hard work was now being left behind in Maidstone. I felt proud of what I had achieved there and felt that I had so much more to give. As the journey progressed, I vowed that wherever they were taking me, I would do my utmost to carry on with the good work. It would probably mean starting from scratch again, but what other choice did I have? It would have been easier to say "Oh well, at least I achieved something at Maidstone" and leave it there, but I was sure that my idea had enough potential to be much bigger and better than it stood at present. My journey concluded and as we pulled up at the prison gates I saw that we were at Coldingley. I was now eighteen years into my life sentence and I was finally downgraded to a Cat C prisoner. I had always been a model prisoner and to be honest, I thought I would have reached Cat C before this point, still I was there now and I was grateful for the easier regime it allowed me.

I was taken to reception and the usual routine followed, my possessions that I'd brought with me had been taken away, including a couple of video tapes of the youth project presentations. I was then searched and issued with my new kit, blankets, toilet pot, mug and knife and fork. I then waited in the corridor outside the office to be allocated to my wing and cell. I stood there for some time as it was lunch time and they were obviously very busy, there were inmates coming and going and as I stood there I glanced across at a notice board, upon which was a printed notice reading "CHAPEL ORDERLY REQUIRED". As I already spent a fair amount of time in the chapel due to my faith, this got my attention immediately and it was a far better option than most of the mind numbingly boring jobs available in most prisons. Eager to keep the job for myself, I positioned myself right in front of the notice, ensuring that as few inmates as possible would see it!

After a while I was finally allocated my wing and cell. Feeling that the Chapel Orderly job would be a popular choice, I requested and filled in the necessary application form and submitted it as soon as I could. A few days later I was called up to the Chapel to see the Chaplain. I assumed that this would be an interview, but as I walked in I noticed there was nobody else around other than the Chaplain, a very nice man named Geoffrey Clarkson. We introduced ourselves and he immediately informed me that the Chaplain Orderly's job was mine and that I was the only applicant, which surprised me. I was astounded that it was that easy. It wasn't long after this that I found out the reason. Coldingley Prison at this time had recently become the first, industrialised prison in the UK and inmates who worked in these type of jobs (predominantly lifers like myself) were earning £100 a week saved up for their release. I didn't know at that time, but I was to be at Coldingley for four years, which would have equated to around £20,000. The Chaplain Orderly's job paid £6 a week.

I have a very strong suspicion that I needn't have gone to the bother of standing in front of the notice board, in an effort to block it out of my fellow inmates' eye-line!

However, I was happy to have been given this opportunity and feel that God had some hand in steering me to it. Also, looking back now, I realise that if I had gone down the industrial work route, I would not have had the necessary time to dedicate to my project. Mr. Clarkson sat me down and over a nice chat and a cup of tea, he explained my duties to me; which consisted of cleaning the Chapel and keeping everything tidy and as it should be. On occasions I would also be saying prayers in services. I told him about my faith and I'm pretty sure he was pleased to have a Christian in the Chaplain Orderly's role. During our chat I also mentioned the work I'd been doing at Maidstone with the youth project and how I'd managed to get it up and running from just a basic idea some years before. He seemed genuinely interested and listened intently as I explained how upset I was at having to leave it all behind. It was only a matter of days later, while I was mopping the foyer entrance to the chapel that Mr. Clarkson entered with the Prison Governor, Mr. John Smith. He introduced me to the Governor, now I had planned to put in an application to see him at some point to ask whether there was a possibility of continuing what I'd started at Maidstone, but feeling that this would be an ideal opportunity strike while the iron was hot, I thought I'd tell him about the youth project and see how he reacted. I needn't have bothered, before I could get more than a couple of words out, he interrupted me, "I know exactly what you're going to ask me Hart...you have my full permission and backing to go ahead". I was astounded, I thought I would have a struggle on my hands getting permission, but it was handed to me on a plate, for which I was very grateful to Mr. Smith and to Reverend Geoffrey Clarkson, who had obviously brought the subject up in conversation. Having the full backing of the Governor just re confirmed my whole confidence and belief in the scheme.

The scheme was implemented immediately, now to be known as The Coldingley Youth Project. I advertised on the notice board for inmates to become involved and was inundated with applicants. Some of these guys were inmates who were previously part of the scheme at Maidstone and had been moved to Coldingley around the same time as myself. However, the vast majority were men who felt they could make a difference.

The chapel at Coldingley consisted of a small worship area and a much larger hall, which was currently being used for educational courses. One of these courses was a well attended drama course, which I felt could be useful as a part of our presentations. With this in mind, I introduced myself to the course tutor, (Bob Taylor) explained what our scheme was about and asked if he'd be willing to incorporate drama into the presentation.

He thought it was a great idea, so we arranged a meeting and sat down with him and some of his drama students and wrote a short play entitled 'Joe's Story". Basically, this play involved two youngsters, names Joe and Mark. Joe asks his father for an Xbox console, his father tells the boy that he can't afford it. So they plan to commit a smash and grab raid on a shop with the consoles displayed in the window. We then see the youngsters outside the shop, Joe asks Mark to get a brick or something to throw through the window. Mark gets hold of a large slab and they commit the robbery.

Then came what we called 'Take 2' where we stop the action at the point of Joe asking Mark to find a brick and then we ask the youngsters in the audience, what Mark can do to stop this robbery progressing any further. The drama tutor thought this would be a great addition to our work and we brought it into action at our very first presentation.

We felt that approaching it this way, making the kids proactive, would engage them far more than just lecturing them about the wrongs of getting involved in criminal activities. It certainly worked, the kids came up with various ideas on how to stop the crime going ahead, we'd then bring them up 'into' the play, (to play Mark) to put their theories to the test. The inmate portraying Joe would then ad-lib and we'd progress from there to see whether their ideas were successful in stopping the crime.

One of the inmates involved in the scheme at that time, was a young guy by the name of Avy. He was an exceptional actor and because of his work on the scheme, he won an award from The Princes Trust. This award was to be presented to him by Angela Palmer, a representative from there. She was so blown away by our work, she became involved shortly afterwards and went on to further success with the scheme as it progressed. (See further chapters).

The scheme went from strength to strength and the inmates were enjoying their work. Bob Taylor was having great success teaching acting skills to the guys involved in the plays, until he came to me one day to tell me that the prison authorities were making him redundant.. This was a real knock-back and I was saddened to hear of this, apparently it was due to financial cut backs. He told me how sad he was to have to leave and was concerned how it would affect The Coldingley Youth Project.

I was determined to do all I could to enable Bob to stay on and asked him if he'd continue if I could finance it. A smile crossed his face, but said that he thought it highly unlikely that an inmate could do this. I carried out some research and applied to the John Paul Getty Trust for a grant and they confirmed that they would be happy to allow us £15,000. This figure was enough to finance Bob's one day a week visits for the next three years.

He was delighted and to say the least, surprised. I was just pleased that the scheme would still have the benefit of his input, as I felt his contributions were invaluable.

As the scheme progressed, I felt we needed some further guidance. So with this in mind, I formed a 'steering committee' consisting of the prison's Head of Education, a probation officer, a representative from an outside body called 'The Safer Surrey Partnership' (with which the scheme formed a partnership which continues to the present day) and other hierarchy from the prison system. This raised the profile of the scheme and from this further funding became available.

Initially, we had a presentation every two months. Shortly after the committee became involved, I was approached by Mr. Smith, the prison Governor, who was pleased to tell me that they would now go ahead on a monthly basis.

The extra money allowed the presentations to be longer and with further content, so we started to bring music back in. Various songs were written, rehearsed and produced with many different crime themes; joyriding, burglary etc. and this brought another level to our work.

During a break in proceedings, the youngsters were taken down to see the segregation unit. We found this brought home to the youngsters just how awful prison can be.

Another new aspect to our work consisted of the youngsters splitting into groups of around six or seven, each group accompanied by two inmates and they could chat. The group leaders, teachers etc. would be outside the room, but still able to see their pupils. This encouraged the kids to talk more openly and on one occasion a young girl confided that a family friend had been sexually abusing her. This matter was obviously reported and subsequently dealt with. She had been unable to talk about this previously, but felt comfortable enough to open up in this scenario. I was certain that the scheme was having much success and that we were managing to do what we had set our minds on, keeping kids away from crime.

On another occasion, the Police brought in a small group of youngsters from Chislehurst in Kent. They were constantly being pulled in by the Police, not attending school, smoking marajuana, snatching handbags, house breaking and generally on the wrong track. PC Ben Lyons brought them in and a short time after our presentation I was pleased to hear from him. He reported that they had gone back to school and had handed in several weapons and tools used for burglary. This proved to me that the scheme was definitely working, we were getting kids back on the straight and narrow. This incident was reported on TV and people were beginning to take notice of The Coldingley Youth Project.

However, I was very upset and saddened to hear that the plug had been pulled on the presentations I'd started back in Maidstone, after one of the youth leaders who brought the youngsters in, had been caught handing over drugs to an inmate. From that point on, I done my best to ensure that the inmates involved were doing it for the right reasons.

My work as the Chapel Orderly continued alongside my activities with the project and I enjoyed my duties there, particularly as I got on so well with Reverend Geoffrey Clarkson. Geoffrey also oversaw the inmate labour force at Coldingley and he was becoming inundated with all of the necessary paperwork, so decided he needed to recruit a capable inmate to take on some of this work. He advertised the job and one of the applicants was an inmate called John Hoskison. Geoffrey realised that the work would present John with no major headaches, so he was taken on.

I warmed to John instantly, he was a very quiet, humble guy and seemed very private. He was a well spoken and intelligent man and to be honest, seemed like a fish out of water there in prison. I asked how he came to be in Coldingley and after some hesitation, he told me his story. He had become a professional golf player at seventeen years of age and he graduated to play for several years on the European Tour alongside such esteemed names as Seve Ballesteros, Nick Faldo and Ian Woosnam. He later became the resident professional at a club back in the UK and was living his ideal life.

After a round of golf with a friend at another course one afternoon, he broke the habit of a lifetime and opted to have a drink. On his drive back home, tragedy struck, he hit a cyclist in a quiet country lane, panicked and drove off. After arriving home, he was so racked with guilt he went to the Police Station and gave himself up. It transpired that the cyclist had subsequently died and John was charged with manslaughter. He was sentenced to three years in prison.

Although our circumstances were totally different, I could totally empathise with John. He felt such guilt over what had occurred as I did myself.

I told him my story and I think he felt we had a common bond of sorts. I'm not for a moment suggesting his actions could be compared in any way to mine, but we had both been responsible for taking a life unintentionally. John was very accepting of his three year sentence and believed that it was totally right and correct that he should be there.

We became close friends and I asked him if he would speak at one of the presentations. He declined, telling me that he didn't feel ready to talk about something that was still so raw in his thoughts. However, he did come along and saw the work that we were doing. After some months of cajoling from me, he relented and told his story at a presentation. Afterwards he confided in me that he felt the experience had been cathartic and that he felt relieved to have spoken of it. Until that point, other than myself, I don't think anybody else inside Coldingley knew the facts behind his incarceration.

John went on to become far more involved in the work of the youth project, eventually taking part in the plays. He was a talented and keen performer. He was always fearful of what life had in store for him after his release, as golf had been his only occupation since school. Doubtful whether that world would ever accept him back after this, he fretted over how he would make a living.

After his release, John was fortunate enough to be able to go back to golf, as well as becoming a successful author of two books, one of which tells of his experiences in prison. He has also spoken to many youngsters over the years since his release, in a somewhat similar capacity to our work on the youth projects. I like to think his experiences with us in Coldingley may have spurred him on!

I have been fortunate to have kept in contact with John over the years and value his friendship greatly.

While working in the prison chapel, one of my other duties was to host a Christian Fellowship meeting every week, where groups of Christians from outside, would come in and pray with and alongside the inmates. One of the regular visitors at these meetings was a lady named Sharon, who played guitar for our Christian songs. I played alongside her and we struck up a friendship which continued throughout the remainder of my sentence and beyond. Pauline who had been brought in to see me during my time in Gartree also continued to come in on occasions, for which I was grateful.

As I mentioned previously, Coldingley was the first industrialised prison in the UK and as such, there were various projects also running there, some of them of an industrial nature. A group of mechanically minded inmates had started a project building motor-tricycles, based around a Volkswagen Beetle rear end with the Chopper style front handlebars. A recycling project was already in full swing at the time and was decreasing the amount of waste needed to go to landfill sites from the prison.

Another fascinating project in operation, was named 'The Bird Project', a group of inmates were breeding and subsequently training birds of prey.

This proved very successful and I found the demonstrations these guys gave with the birds enthralling. They were beautiful creatures and to see them in full flight was a thing of beauty.

As a tribute to the success of these projects in Coldingley, a stain glass window had been installed in the chapel depicting all of them and it remains there to this day.

On occasions, a guest speaker would be invited in give a talk to the Prison Fellowship in the church hall, usually on a subject the authorities felt would be of interest to the inmates. At one of these, the guest speak was to be the ex- inmate Chris, at whose hands I'd suffered that beating in Albany some years previously. Since then, Chris had become a born again Christian while inside and had since been released. His conversion to Christianity had occurred in circumstances not dissimilar to mine, in that it happened at a time of despair, in prison, during a life sentence. Chris came in and gave his talk which I genuinely found very inspiring and despite what had happened between us years earlier, I felt a bond with the man through our Christianity. As the talk finished, I made my way over to speak with him. I offered my hand and asked if he remembered me. He shook my hand and apologised for not being able to recall where we had met. When I refreshed his memory, he looked horrified to be reminded of this and I told him that I was a Christian now and that I forgave him. His eyes filled with tears and we hugged. It was quite a moment, Chris does some great work within the church to this day and I wish him well

I celebrated (if you can call it that) my 60th birthday during my time at Coldingley and on that day, being quite a milestone in anybody's life, it made me think back to the start of my sentence all those years earlier. Here I was, fast approaching my 'Autumn years' and I was a relatively young man when I was first locked up. I had kept myself fit and took pride in my general appearance, but there was no getting away from the fact, I was now of a certain vintage that is widely considered 'old'!

As a lifer, I didn't really know when this sentence would end. I had been given life, with a recommended minimum of twenty-five years. On my 60th birthday, I had been inside for twenty years and seven months, my children (of which the eldest was fifteen when I went away) were all now adults well into their thirties and I was a grandfather to four boys and two girls!

I had been on a massive journey over those twenty years and as I looked back, I felt that I had improved as a person. Prison is meant to rehabilitate, however it attracts much criticism for failing on this score. Personally, I felt it had been successful. I realise that no amount of time behind bars can ever bring back that poor young lady who died all those years ago, but I hope that all my efforts during my time inside has shown how much I regret what happened and how much I want to make a difference. I also feel, that the inmates who have become involved in the youth crime diversion schemes in Coldingley and Maidstone have also become better people as a result of their participation. I'm nobody's fool and I realise that initially, some inmates became involved in the projects as a means of scoring 'brownie points' to aid an early release. However, once they saw how successful they were being in helping those kids by steering them away from trouble, they soon realised that it was so worthwhile.

In 1998 the project won our first Award, this was from The British Crime Prevention and Community Safety Awards. This award was put up by Crime Concern, CGU Insurance and the Home Office. Highly Commending Coldingley Prison Youth Project and Safer Surrey Partnership for their effective partnership solution to the prevention of everyday crime in their community. The Home Secretary at the time was

Rt. Hon. Jack Straw MP who signed the award. In March 1999 Richard Stilgo, who was the High Sheriff of Surrey at the time, gave the scheme our second Award. This was to the Coldingley Youth Project in recognition of great and valuable services to the community. KeepOut at Coldingley has gone on to win many other High Sheriffs awards over the years.

It was a proud time for me, it made me realise what can be achieved if one put's one's mind to it. A spark of an idea all those years ago had come to this. I'm proud to say that this was the first in a long line of awards to be won and we continue to win awards to this day. I was also honoured to be introduced Princess Anne on one occasion while visiting the prison and she took great interest in our work.

I was attending to some business in the church one day, when I had a visit from a female SO, (Senior Officer) who had come along to inform me that I was to be downgraded to Cat D and that I would soon be moved to Ford Open Prison. This came totally out of the blue and the news hit me like a sledgehammer. Finally I could see some light at the end of the tunnel. I was obviously delighted and without thinking what I was doing, jumped up and hugged and kissed this lovely lady who had given me the best news I'd had in years! She reprimanded me for my behaviour, but I could see that she was doing her best to smother her amusement, as a wry smile came over her face.

I had made preparations for the young inmate Avy, who I mentioned earlier to take over the project after my transfer and he managed this wonderfully, supervising the twenty-five inmates on the project.

Shortly after this I was moved from Coldingley after four years, sad in some ways to be leaving the scheme, my work and my friends behind, but also glad to be progressing through my sentence.

CHAPTER TWENTY FOUR
FORD - THE LAST STRETCH

Ford is an open prison near the pretty town of Arundel in West Sussex. It was formerly a Fleet Air Arm base and was converted to a prison in 1960. It is a Cat D prison and as such, caters for prisoners serving short sentences or those reaching the tail end of longer sentences, such as myself.

My journey from Coldingley was in one of the old style 'Black Maria's' which surprised me as I thought they had been fazed out in favour of the newer white transportation vehicles. The cubicles in these vehicles were cramped and seemed to create a stifling atmosphere if the temperature was anything over freezing. However, I was hardly in a position to complain, so suffered my uncomfortable surroundings for what was, thankfully a relatively short trip.

I had now been in prison for close on twenty-three years. At my sentencing, I was given life with a recommendation that I serve a minimum of twenty-five years. However, as a lifer, there was no automatic release upon completion of those twenty five years. I was not to find out a release date until very close to the actual day, unlike the majority of prisoners. If you're given five years, you know your release date from day one of your sentence, (dependent on behaviour etc) whereas for someone in my position, it's almost all down to 'let's see how it goes'. I feel as though I had always been a decent person while inside and just got my head down and got on with it.

Even though my appeal had failed all those years ago, I was still determined to somehow prove that I had not intentionally fired the gun on the robbery. Occasionally, at that late stage of my sentence, I had questioned myself as whether it was all too late and whether there would be any point. Even now, writing this book, at seventy six years of age, I still haven't put the thought of another appeal entirely to bed. However, each time I think of another appeal, the remorse I've felt from day one seems to drown out the word 'appeal', then I'm reluctant to continue. Even after all this time, the remorse is still very strong.

Upon arrival at Ford, everybody follows an induction course and during this time is placed in a single room (no cells at Ford!) Even though I had been using a computer for some time at Coldingley while carrying out business for the scheme, my skills were rather limited as I only really knew what I had taught myself through bumbling through.

Therefore, I opted to take an available course there, entitled 'Computer Literacy and Information Technology', which I enjoyed immensely. During my studies, I realised that some of the habits I had picked up while 'winging it' on the computer at Coldingley, were rather long winded and much shorter, more efficient methods were available to me. The course lasted six weeks and I considered it to be very comprehensive, I learnt an awful lot in that time and I was an enthusiastic pupil. I sat an exam upon completion of the course and thankfully passed with flying colours. My new skills would certainly prove useful in my future work with the scheme, that's for sure.

During this time, my mind was still very active in thinking of new ideas I could incorporate into the presentations and even though I had actually left the scheme behind me as a working charity at Coldingley, I was determined that I would continue with my work in a similar vein, in one way or another. I made initial enquiries upon arrival as to whether it would be possible for me to continue with the scheme there, however this was turned down, which disappointed me, but there was nothing I could do to change the Governor's mind, so I had to accept it for the time being. I never found the Governor at Ford to be in the slightest bit interested in trying to help anyone. He seemed as though he would just do his job and absolutely no more. I asked him when I arrived whether he would give his backing for me to petition the Home Secretary, for a reduction in my sentence tariff and he turned me down flat.

His general attitude to his work surprised me to be honest, Ford is meant to be a place where long termers are prepared to re-enter society and he didn't take the slightest interest in this endeavour. I found out (albeit at a much later date) his reasoning behind his reluctance in getting behind my endeavours with the crime diversion scheme; he had signed the papers allowing a lifer out to work in an old people's home during the day and they found out this inmate had been convicted of murder and complained, so I suppose I could see why he would be overly cautious.

I signed up for two NVQ courses which I passed convincingly some weeks later,in painting/decorating and building carpentry. These had obviously been part of my trade before this sentence and it was quite basic, but after such a long time away from the tools, I didn't think it would be in the slightest bit harmful to have my memory refreshed. I passed both with ease.

After a sort qualifying time at Ford, most inmates were required to work in some capacity or another, mainly in an actual job outside of the prison. I was initially employed at a nearby sewage farm, not the most pleasant of working environments, it has to be said but it was okay and to be honest, I just enjoyed the experience of being outside after such a long time behind bars.

There are theories as to how long a man can be incarcerated before his mental state is affected; I have seen twelve years being mooted on more than one occasion as the maximum before changes are expected. I had now served almost twice this time and I considered myself to still be in full use of all my faculties, however some may disagree! I jest, but seriously, I have witnessed first-hand the way some men change during their sentences. I'm not for one moment suggesting that I was the same man that entered prison twenty-three years earlier, to think that I hadn't changed in some ways would be unrealistic, I had changed, but hopefully I had changed for the better. I felt a better man for the work that I had carried out and also for living a Christian life.

I feel a major factor in remaining sane throughout a long sentence, is to keep one's mind active. Endless hours of meaningless, day-time TV takes it's toll. Watching that drivel, hour after hour does not stimulate your brain cells one iota. You need to constantly challenge yourself and I'm pretty sure all my endeavours with this purpose paid off. My work with the debating societies, which progressed to the crime diversion scheme, my Braillist duties, my craft and woodworking hobbies and my work within the church all contributed to my mental well being, I'm fairly certain of that. As you've read previously, my fitness had always been important too and even though I was now the wrong side of sixty, I could still give most men fifteen years younger than me a run for their money on the track! A healthy body = a healthy mind they say, I agree whole heartedly.

My work at the sewage farm lasted for three months and I enjoyed it. I had always worked hard in my trade, prior to my life sentence, even while I was active criminally and had never been afraid to get stuck in and my enthusiasm continued now.

An inmate who I'd become friendly with, told me he could put me forward for a similar job to his, which was at The Arun Yacht Club. I thought he was having a laugh, surely an upmarket establishment like a yacht club wouldn't employ cons? However, he was serious and I managed to secure an interview, after which I was offered the position.

A requirement of the job, was that each employee had to have a bank account for wages to be paid into and obviously after such a long time inside, I did not. Therefore, two screws took five of us down to Ford Town in an effort to open accounts for us inmates. One entered the bank and we watched as he spoke to the clerk. The screw in the van with us, told us that if they agreed to opening an account, he'd give the thumbs up as he left the building. Fortunately we all got the thumbs up, so all was good and I started at the Arun Yacht Club.

Initially, I was employed there as a cleaner and as much as I enjoyed the work, I felt I was capable of much more. After a short while there, the club committee purchased a mobile home which they intended to convert into a training centre and I put myself forward, telling them that I was very capable of carrying out the conversion. Thankfully, they had confidence in my abilities and I set to the task. I removed all the interior walls, put a little, fitted kitchenette in and generally made a classroom from it. I was proud of my work and the hierarchy at the club seemed impressed too.

Throughout my time in Ford, Sharon who I'd met at the Christian Fellowship Meetings in Coldingley, continued to visit me and our friendship grew stronger still. There's no way it could be classed as a romance, considering my circumstances, but if things were different, it probably would have been.

During my time in Coldingley, I had met a kindly Vicar from Brighton, by the name of Len Merrett, who used to visit youngsters in prison in an effort to get them to change their ways and to keep on the straight and narrow upon release. I first met him on one of his visits while he waited in the Chapel and I had served him tea and biscuits. He had explained to me about his work and efforts, working with the younger inmates and then I had obviously told him about the crime diversion scheme that I had started. He showed great interest in my work and now I was in Ford, we had still maintained contact.

He decided that he wanted to involve me in his work and after much letter writing and representations, he had managed to persuade the authorities to release me on a daily basis to help him. He had rented an office in Brighton and had named the new scheme 'Chapter International' (25:36) this name coming from a piece of text from the bible;

Mathew, Chapter 25 : 35. For I was hungry, and you gave me something to eat; I was thirsty, and you gave me something to drink; I was a stranger, and you invited me in; 36. naked, and you clothed me; I was sick, and you visited me; I was in prison, and you came to me.

I began travelling down to Brighton on a daily basis and had been given the run of the office, equipped with telephones and computer and we began to get the scheme up and running. After work each day, I boarded the train back to Ford Prison.

All went well and we were making some great progress. I was glad to be doing something useful and in many ways, it was a sort of continuation of the work that I had started in Coldingley.

Len made applications on my behalf (which the Ford Prison Governor had refused to do) to the then Home Secretary, Jack Straw, in an effort to get a reduction on my sentence, and very soon afterwards we were informed that Mr. Straw had recommended that a year be taken from my tariff, for exceptional behaviour during my sentence. As by this time, I had served approximately a year in Ford, I was very hopeful that I would be released very soon. All the paperwork that Len had received from the Home Office was submitted to a dedicated unit within Ford Prison that dealt with issues solely pertaining to 'lifers' such as myself and we waited to hear some good news. After sweating it out for some time with no response from them, we made enquiries as to what was occurring with my case. A considerable time passed and we still heard nothing. Upon further enquiries, they finally came back to inform us that as I was on a two year program to be reintegrated back into community, nothing could be done about my release until that two year program had been completed.

I was livid, how could an individual clerical worker within Ford Prison overrule the Home Secretary Mr. Jack Straw. I made my objections to the 'Lifer Unit' very clear and asked them the same question. Also, why didn't they at the very least, have the decency to inform me of their decision as soon as the original paperwork was submitted to them, rather than no response at all. I literally had to force them to make any response at all.

I was determined that I wasn't going to take this without a fight, so I made applications to be granted legal aid in an effort to have this decision overturned. The necessary paperwork was submitted and I waited.....and waited. All the usual red tape of these things was taking even more time, time that as far as Mr. Jack Straw and I were concerned, should have been MY time, time that I should be spending at home.

Eventually the gears and cogs at Legal Aid ground to a halt and they came back to me with their decision, 'Legal Aid not granted'. To be honest with myself, I don't really think now, looking back, that I could have expected anything other than this. At the time I was desperate to get out as soon as possible and was grasping at every opportunity, who wouldn't be? However, I still find it incredible that the Home Secretary's recommendation could be overruled like that.

I tried my best to put this disappointment to the back of my mind and continued with my work in Brighton with Chapter International. I had been given the title Head Office Coordinator, very grand for a prisoner still serving a life sentence.

Len obviously knew how successful my original crime diversion scheme in Coldingley had been and continued to be, in helping youngsters BEFORE they offended. Whereas at this time Chapter International were there solely to help offenders AFTER the criminal misdemeanour, he saw the potential in expanding his work to incorporate the Coldingley scheme's mission statement.

With this in mind, he proposed to start Chapter International Youth Crime Diversion Scheme with me spearheading operations. I was thrilled that Len had shown this confidence in me to take this task on for him.

He brought in a Solicitor to deal with all the necessary legalities of becoming a registered charity and within six weeks this was completed and we were up and running.

My initial duties consisted of contacting schools, Youth Offending Teams, Pupil Referral Units and the Police to inform them of our existence and what we were proposing to do. I had extremely positive replies from everybody, with the Police promising to donate £5,000 and M & S £2,000, as soon as the visits and presentations to the youngsters commenced. This was great news and really brought it home to me just how much potential there was in my original idea that I'd had all those years early. Within weeks more donations came in and we were really going places.

During this period of day release down to Brighton, my Probation Officer was obviously very much on top of all my activities and as I was nearing the end of my sentence, we were formatting a release plan. Basically this consisted in putting together all the details of how my life was to progress after my eventual release. The first necessary condition of release is a fixed and stable address. Obviously, as I had been divorced from Wendy for many years, there was no marital home to go back to, so my son David had agreed that I was to live with him in Basingstoke, until I was in a position to find my own accommodation. The Probation Officer was fine with this arrangement and also with my proposal to continue my work with Len Merrett and Chapter International in Brighton for three days a week and to spend the other four days in Basingstoke. Things were shaping up nicely and I looked forward to my release.

I had served just short of two and a half years in Ford when I was given the news of my release. I was informed three weeks in advance, the date was 6th June 2002. After more than twenty five years inside, I was finally going to be a free man. It was amazing to know I would be walking out of the gates of Ford Prison within twenty one days. In some ways, I wish they had told me just the day before. At least then, I would have been given the news, gone to bed and then..bosh, out, but there I was, counting the days and twenty one days dragged! That might sound strange, "what's twenty one days after serving over twenty five years", you might ask, but believe me, it seemed far, far more than three weeks to me.

The final arrangements for my release were made and I began to say my goodbyes to friends I'd made in Ford. That much awaited day finally arrived and I left prison for the last time. I was certain in my mind that I would never serve another sentence. I almost worded that sentence 'never set foot in a prison again', but that would not be true, as my work with the scheme in the years following my release, was to bring me back into various prisons on a regular basis.

CHAPTER TWENTY FIVE
OUT

I was now sixty-four years of age and I had been in prison for more than thirty one of those. I had been sentenced to more than 125 years in total, (most of those were served concurrently). Almost half my life to that point, had been spent in prison. Anyway, there's a famous saying, 'it's no use crying over spilt milk', the fact of the matter was, I was out, ready to start again with the £47 release money handed to me!

When I look back now I realise how much I missed during that time; I'd missed the birth of some of my kids, I'd missed their very early years and I had missed their move from childhood through their teenage years and into adulthood. In effect, I had not been there for their lives to the point I was released from the life sentence and for that I am so sorry. A child's upbringing is an important part of their lives, it makes them who they are and I wasn't there for it. I'm sure there are many reading this who would say, (considering who and what I was during that period of my life), perhaps I wouldn't have been the best influence and I wouldn't really be able to put up too good an argument. However, I'm pretty certain that I wouldn't have made the mistakes that my parents made by actively encouraging me to become a criminal. My kids, although I hadn't been there, had been brought up wonderfully and were well rounded, nice people and for that I have to thank my dear ex-wife Wendy. She had been put into an almost impossibly difficult situation by me and somehow she managed to still make a fantastic job of everything. My lifestyle choices had ruined my marriage and for that, I am also so sorry. How Wendy managed to stay married to me for as long as she did, I'll never know and I am eternally grateful to her. By the time of my release, she had met a lovely guy who she is with to this day and I couldn't be happier for them. The lady is a total saint in my eyes and remains a very good friend.

On my release from Ford on the 6th June 2002, my 'kids', Jane, David and Lucy were 40, 39 and 38 years old respectively and I had a lot of making up to do and I was determined to make the most of my life from that point onwards, however I was well aware that nothing I could do would actually bring back all that time away from my family.

I was picked up from Ford by Sharon and we drove to Basingstoke, where she dropped me off at David's house, which was to be my home for the next six months. I made arrangements to see Sharon later that week, after I'd settled in. Later that day, my daughters came round to see me with all my grandchildren. As mentioned previously, I now had six, Adam, Ryan, Ann, Jack, Ian and Kate, ranging from five years old up to fifteen. It was all a bit surreal at first and my first night in a proper bed, in a proper bedroom was strange!

I had to attend an appointment with my probation officer the very next day after my release, at their office in Basingstoke. Obviously, the main point of discussion was to be my plans for the future and I re-iterated my desire to continue my work with Chapter International in Brighton. The probation service had been well aware from my pre-release meetings in Ford, that I planned to work in Brighton for three days and spend the remaining four days of the week in Basingstoke at my son David's house and had raised no objection. However, at this first appointment the officer said that it would create too much work for them and that it would not be possible, reasoning that for my three days in Brighton I would have to be transferred to the care of the Sussex probation service and then re-transferred back to Hampshire probation service every week when I returned to Basingstoke. I objected strongly to this and told them that my plans had been put before them during my pre-release meetings in Ford, but they wouldn't back down. As far as I could see, their only reason for not allowing me to work in Brighton was their laziness. How difficult could it possibly be?

I was determined that I wouldn't let a setback like this put me off and set about finding a way around this obstacle.

On my first weekend back in Basingstoke, my kids laid on a beautiful party for me. It was a lovely gesture and I enjoyed myself immensely. I found it very emotional being surrounded by so many friends and family, that had stood by me throughout my turbulent life. It would have been so easy for them to have abandoned me, especially my kids, as they had been through so much. I know from what Wendy told me during the early part of my life sentence, that they had suffered taunts from their peers at school. If anyone had the right to feel bitter about what had been bestowed upon them due to my actions, it was my kids, but they were there for me and completely non judgemental.

Although (aside from the knock back from the probation service regarding my continuation to work with Chapter International), I planned to carry on with my crime diversion work with youngsters in whatever capacity I could, at that immediate time, I still needed to earn a living. I was sixty-four years of age, not too far shy of 'retirement' age, but I wasn't about to sit back and take things easy, I was still very fit and eager to get going again.

I started looking around to see what opportunities there were in the building trade. As mentioned earlier in this book, I had always worked hard (mainly in the building game) throughout my life, despite my criminal activities and had kept my skills fresh with courses during my sentence.

Within two weeks of leaving prison, I was working back in my trade on a self-employed basis and it gave me a real sense of pride to be earning a living again. It may sound such a trivial matter, but to come out of prison at sixty four years of age, after serving a life sentence and be working again within such a short period of time meant the world to me.

Once I had been working for a few weeks, I thought it would be a nice gesture to take my ex-wife Wendy and her husband out to a show and a meal. Hardly fair recompense for all the hardship and grief I'd put her through over the years, but I felt I needed to show her that I was grateful for what she had done. Fortunately, she was agreeable and we all enjoyed a pleasant evening. I remain on good terms with her and her husband to this day and see them both quite regularly.

I continued to see Sharon regularly and our relationship flourished into a full on romance, as I expected it would. Throughout my first year after my release, we began to make plans for our life together and we discussed the possibility of me moving in with her. This all sounded great and as much as I really liked Sharon, she wasn't the easiest lady in the world to get on with, she could be quite demanding. Having said that, I don't suppose I was totally blameless. After twenty-five years inside, it was probably no picnic for her either. However, for a few years after my release, our relationship continued until I decided that I wanted to leave my work in the building trade and concentrate on my crime diversion work on a full time basis. I told Sharon of my plans and she wasn't best pleased, I was earning decent money with my building work by this stage and she didn't relish the thought of losing the comfortable lifestyle that would allow. I think the final straw came when she said to me while discussing my plans, "you didn't ask me". Anyway, our relationship ended there and then unfortunately.

I had obviously informed Len Merrett from Chapter International, of the probation service's objections to me working alongside him in Brighton and he was as upset as I was at their sudden change of heart. He couldn't fathom how they could go back on their word. He was determined that I would continue to work alongside him somehow and with this in mind we formed Youth Crime Solutions (YCS), working within Chapter International's due restriction.

I had managed to buy myself an old Ford Escort as a runaround and I used that to drive to Guildford Cathedral and meet Len Merrett for regular meetings to discuss our activities. However, my old banger wasn't the best vehicle on the road and began to let me down, so Len very kindly gave me a Peugeot 406 as he was about to upgrade to a later model. This was a company car belonging to Chapter International and he realised that I needed a good, reliable car for my ongoing activities within the company. I was now visiting many schools, giving talks to the youngsters, telling them my story and hopefully, keeping them on the straight and narrow, exactly what I had envisaged doing all those years ago in Coldingley.

Approximately six months after being released, I managed to secure a little flat from Basingstoke Council. I was so appreciative to have been given this opportunity. It was a lovely little place, not grand by any means, but it was my own front door and I continue to live there to the present day.

My son David had been great, but I didn't want to impose on his family life any longer than was absolutely necessary.

I had been told before my release, that once I had managed to secure my own accommodation, I would be able to apply for a grant to help me furnish it. As soon as I'd been offered and accepted the council flat, I submitted all the necessary forms and papers to apply for the grant, however as is the way with all these type of things, I waited and waited but heard nothing. Eventually, the day arrived for me to move into my new place and I'd still heard nothing of my grant, therefore as I had managed to save enough to furnish it to a basic level, I purchased my requirements myself. Shortly afterwards, the people responsible for the grant contacted me and asked what I needed for my flat. I explained that as I had already moved in and rather than move in with absolutely no furniture, I had purchased the goods etc. at my own expense. They responded with a curt "Well then, you don't need a grant". I thought I would be reimbursed and had kept all the receipts to show them, apparently not. As I had somehow scraped the money together myself to buy the furniture, it was deemed that I didn't need the grant. It seems my honesty had cost me a lot of money!

However, what was done was done, at least I had my own little place which was within easy reach of all my kids, so I continued to see them on a regular basis. I set about doing my utmost to make my little flat a home.

All in all, everything was going so well for the next couple of years. I was enjoying my crime diversion work with YCS and was managing to keep my head above water, although not by any stretch of the imagination, was I in the lap of luxury.

I had kept in contact with Pauline regularly since getting out and now that my relationship with Sharon had ended, we began to see more of each other. This progressed into a romance and she was a lovely lady. She took me on a holiday to Kuala Lumpur, which should have been the holiday of a lifetime. Unfortunately poor Pauline was mugged twice during the holiday which put a bit of a damper on the whole thing.

I'd noticed on one of my regular meetings with Len Merrett that he was not looking at all well. I didn't like to mention anything to him, but his appearance worried me. Shortly afterwards, I wasn't that surprised to find out that he had been admitted to hospital, but I was startled to hear just how serious his condition actually was. He was due to have open heart surgery and unfortunately it didn't work out for him and he passed away.

His passing upset me a great deal as I liked Len immensely. He was a lovely man and had shown a great deal of faith in me. Unfortunately, Len had left no instructions or provision in his will as to the future of Chapter International and Len's son, Andrew had no intention of carrying on with any of Chapter's work. Andrew contacted me shortly after his father's death, informing me that he wanted the Peugeot back. I told him that Len had in fact, given me the car. He told me that if I wanted to keep it, I'd need to pay him £5,700. I said that there was some cash in Chapter's account that I had managed to raise, however he said that that had been given away elsewhere.

Eventually, I came to an arrangement with him to pay the cash back as I needed the car. This whole affair was very upsetting, I missed Len as a friend and a colleague and now I was back to square one again, as far as my crime diversion work was concerned and a lot lighter in pocket too. As I had been working under Chapter's title, without their financial backing and good will, I'd have to find another avenue for my work.

Not wanting to leave it too long, I set about looking for other opportunities immediately. I remembered a chap called Brian Sinclair had come into Coldingley during my time there, on a Christian Ministry mission and during his talk, he spoke of a charity that he ran called 'The Door UK', their main mission being to help prisoners upon their release. I thought that my YCS work may be of interest to him, so contacted him and asked if we could meet to discuss this possibility.

This meeting went very well and we formed an agreement where I would work under Door UK's banner as YCS. I began to help with fundraising and was quite successful in this task, securing donations from various bodies and making some very useful contacts, including the Police in Winchester and Southampton, who would refer me to schools and organisations that would benefit from my crime diversion work and presentations.

This continued and as far as I was aware, all was well. Unfortunately, unbeknown to me, Brian had some personal problems that he had managed to keep to himself, however it eventually came out that 'The Door UK' was struggling financially as a result.

I didn't want to see his charity go under and all my hard work go to waste again, so I invested some cash into the charity, hopeful that it would tide them over and out of the hole they were in. Unfortunately, it was too little, too late and Brian's charity folded.

Fortunately, over the last few months of my work within The Door UK, I had made contact again with Angela Palmer. Angela was the representative from The Princes Trust, who had seen and been so impressed with one of our presentations in Coldingley, that she had become involved with The Coldingley Youth Project, (which by this time had been renamed The Coldingley Crime Diversion Scheme, CCDS) and was now the Chief Executive Officer (CEO). As mentioned in previous chapters, when I left Coldingley, I was sorry to leave the youth project behind, but with Angela at the wheel now, they had gone from strength to strength. I approached Angela with a view to carry on my YCS work with the charity and she was delighted to welcome me back to the charity that I'd started all those years before.

Within a short time, I was up and running again and was honoured to be awarded the title of 'Founder' of KeepOut.

In addition to my regular work of talking to youngsters on my YCS scheme, I was now attending and participating in the presentations in Coldingley Prison. It felt rather strange on my first visit there, knowing that I was going in again, but even more strange that I knew I was coming back out again within a few hours!

On one of my visits there, I noticed that they were now bringing young girls in to the presentations. When I started this, it was just young lads attending and the thought occurred to me that maybe this could be expanded into a women's prison. I felt that young girls would be able to fully relate to the experiences of female inmates, rather than to those of male prisoners. After the meeting, I mulled the idea over in my mind and the more I thought about it, the better idea it seemed. I drove over to Angela's house to put my ideas forward.

Angela was not slow at getting things moving. She called me a couple of months later and informed me that the launch of KeepOut at HMP Send was taking place in May 2008. She had done an incredible amount of work in a short time, convincing the governor at Send, and the Home Office that this scheme would be an asset to this women's prison. She had managed to persuade them that there were many teenage girls (at risk of offending) who would be better served attending a presentation at a woman's prison, rather than being taken to Coldingley men's prison a few miles away. The scheme had now been re-named 'KeepOut The Crime Diversion Scheme', as this combined both prisons under the same name.

This had been on her mind for quite a while, she wanted to change the project name but could not think of anything suitable. She was at home one day with the radio on and a particular song caught her attention. The chorus of the song was repeating "keep out, keep out". This gave her the idea of joining the words 'keep' and 'out' together to make 'KeepOut The Crime Diversion Scheme'.

Strangely enough, the amusing anecdote concerning Angela's epiphany moment of hearing the tune on the radio, was that the tune that she heard, which was called "Le Freak" by Chic and the chorus actually said FREAK Out and not KEEP Out! So Angela's mishearing of the lyrics to "Le Freak" is responsible for the charity's new name of 'KeepOut'..

As I worked for the next few years on my Youth Crime Solutions project, Angela was continually busy behind the scenes. Her work load had increased from being CEO for two prison schemes instead of one. This did not stop her from looking into getting a third scheme started at another suitable prison.

On the 1st October 2011 the official launch of KeepOut took place at HMP Lewes. I have nothing but absolute respect for Angela in achieving this, as the work involved in doing this is vast. Before anything can be initiated, permission needs to be granted by the various people and authorities for the scheme to go ahead. Then the laborious task of advertising for and interviewing civilians to fill the roles of operation manager and support worker. Once this is done, advertising for inmates, and selecting the right candidates to be trained for the scheme. This wasn't always an easy process as some inmates who have since worked on the prison scheme have had to be given fairly basic training in Maths and English. Once their training is completed, the security officers in the prison have to lay down some basic rules for the operation. Suitable dates for the presentations then have to be arranged. While this has been going on contact has to be made with the various user groups. Schools, Colleges, local Youth Offending Teams, the police and probation service.

I attended the launch and we were all welcomed by the Governor Robin Eldridge. I gave my speech, as did our CEO Angela. The newly appointed Operation Manager Angela Murray spoke as if she had been doing this forever. Then it was over to the now fully trained inmates to give a demonstration of their newly acquired skills. This was finished with closing remarks from our President Penelope Keith CBE. The whole launch had run as smooth as silk, as if it had had many rehearsals, which it had not.

The audience consisted of many dignitaries and VIPs including the local Mayor, the High Sheriffs of east and west Sussex, and the leaders of all the user groups, as mentioned previously. After Penelope had finished speaking the rapturous applaud lasted for a full two minutes. I felt most of this applaud should have been for Angela Palmer, she had worked tirelessly over a long time to get this amazing launch to take place so perfectly.

Now with three KeepOut schemes running in three different prisons, our CEO told me on many occasions she was exhausted and would have to get some help. Unbeknown to me at that time she was arranging for the scheme to open in another prison, however, at that time, a location had yet to be decided on. Brixton, having a high incidence of crime, finally became her choice.

As mentioned early on in this book, HMP Brixton was where I had served my first custodial sentence and I knew from personal experience that it would be no easy job to implement our work there. However, Angela pressed on regardless and eventually made all of the same preparations she had made at Send and Lewes for this next challenge. The launch of the KeepOut Crime Diversion Scheme at HMP Brixton was on the 11th October 2013. Massive amounts of work had gone into this by a now very tired Angela. Nothing was forgotten and the launch was just as successful as the one at HMP Lewes. My admiration of Angela for her tireless work, organisational skills and patience is of the highest order.

The latest KeepOut Annual Review for the year ended 31 March 2014 is an enlightening document. During 2013 - 2014 the statistics show 233 groups of teenagers have attended the four prison schemes. These young people, most who were on the cusp of offending, were all from the south east of England. Over 1800 teenagers have benefitted from the inmates presentations. Before the KeepOut scheme started most of these inmates would have been either unemployed or doing mundane jobs within the prison. Not only do the young people benefit from this scheme but the inmates also.

Successive governments have failed to have much impact on prisoner rehabilitation. KeepOut have the proud record of helping hundreds of inmates in their own rehabilitation. Many registered charities applied for the Robin Corbett Award For Prisoner Rehabilitation, the KeepOut scheme were the winners. Robin Corbett was an MP who was passionate about penal reform, he believed a jail sentence should not be about society's revenge, but rather the chance to change the direction of a life.

As mentioned earlier, I was released from prison in 2002 and have never reoffended. Twelve of these thirteen years, I have ran my Youth Crime Solutions project. Around forty thousand teenagers have attended these educational crime diversion sessions. I would like to think I have been successful in turning young lives around for the better. During these sessions, I always use, as an example, my own involvement in committing petty offences at a young age and as I grew older, getting more deeply drawn into more serious crime. I then tell them of myself spending over twenty five years in prison where I was stabbed, beaten up and had a pretty awful time. The majority of the young people I spoke to were sixteen years of age or younger. The feedback I received from these sessions was positive and really encouraged me in my endeavours.

Three other inmates who were part of the KeepOut scheme at HMP

Coldingley have also shown how it was this that helped in their own rehabilitation. After their release each one started their own crime diversion schemes that are still operating today. The first in South London called Foundation for Life. the second The Birmingham Crime Diversion Scheme. And thirdly Youth Empowerment Plus in Leatherhead.

Many other ex-inmates who were members of the KeepOut scheme have not only won Awards but have been given jobs with Youth Offending Teams, or are working in the community on projects helping to stop youngsters from following in their footsteps in to prison.

Any charity will tell you of the problems it has in raising sufficient funds to continue with the service they provide. In the early days I had to raise the funds to keep our small project running. Today, with our scheme running in four different locations we have to raise around four hundred thousand pounds per year. Fortunately we have an extremely brilliant fund raiser, James Marlow, who has now been with us for over ten years and does a terrific job. We are most thankful to all of the grant giving trusts who have supported us over the years.

With everything taken into account, it costs us as a charity, approximately one hundred pounds to process one young person, the whole purpose being to keep them out of prison. We have been very successful in doing this over many years. If a young person (aged fifteen or under) gets a custodial sentence it costs the government one hundred and forty thousand pounds a year to keep them in a Young Offenders Institution.

As I write this, I have been out of prison for twelve and a half years and although it has gone so quickly, I like to feel that I have used the time constructively.

Nothing I do could ever fully repay the debt I owe for my actions, but I have done everything I can, not because I feel I had to, but because I wanted to. If my various crime diversion endeavours has meant that some youngsters have managed to stay out of prison and away from an existence anything like mine, then my work has been worthwhile.

Since my release, the thought of raising some sort of an appeal again, against my conviction for murder has never been too far from my thoughts. At one point, a wealthy acquaintance of mine was prepared to help me finance putting something together, unfortunately these plans fell through and I was back to square one. Realistically, at this stage of my life and after such a long time, I don't suppose this plan will ever come to fruition, but there's nothing I wish for more than being able to prove that I did not intend firing that gun all those years earlier.

IN CONCLUSION

For several years after my release, the thought of myself ever laying down in print any sort of document detailing my rather eventful life never occurred to me. Upon release, at the rather senior age of sixty-four, I was determined to put (as best as I could) everything behind me and make an entirely fresh start. However, this was easier said than done. My work within KeepOut (www.crimediversionscheme.org.uk) occupies much of my time, but inevitably there are times when my mind drifts back and I try to make some sort of sense of my actions throughout my life. Once again, this was easier said than done.

I've mentioned my dysfunctional upbringing many times throughout this book, was this to blame for who I became? Was it just fate? Are our lives mapped out for us from day one and there's nothing we can do about the route they take? Who knows?

However, there is one thing I am fairly certain of; at the time in that freezing cell in Long Lartin prison, when I was at an all time low, suicidal, naked and shaking uncontrollably with the extreme cold, when I called out for help and nobody came, I wanted to be shown another way and I truly believe what occurred was God showing me another way. My life changed from that point and I feel it changed for the better. Maybe that was the way my life was mapped out for me, again who knows? Whatever the reason, I feel God had some hand in the way my life has progressed.

Since my release I have been fortunate enough to travel to some wonderful parts of the world, including Australia, where I spent some time on the beautiful Bondi Beach. While soaking up the sun, my mind drifted back again to that dreadful cell where I doubted whether I'd ever see the ocean again and yet there I was, on what many consider the best beach in the world. I like to think God had some hand in helping me achieve this as well.

I am still very active within the church and my Christianity means an awful lot to me. It has helped me come to terms with my life and made me realise that my story may possibly be of help and inspiration to other people and to this end, this book was written. Over countless hours, countless cups of coffee and microwave curries, I have poured out my heart to Keith, who has made some sense of my memories and hopefully we have made a readable story.

In some small way, if it can give hope and inspiration to those who feel they are beyond hope and inspiration, then this book has served it's purpose.

I thank you for taking the time to read it.

Keith How and Mick Hart 2015